REPRIEVE FROM WAR

by the same author:

THE RISE OF ANGLO-AMERICAN FRIENDSHIP
(1938)

PEACE BY POWER
(1942)

LIONEL GELBER

REPRIEVE

FROM WAR

A Manual for Realists

TORONTO

The Macmillan Company of Canada Limited

1950

for
Sylva,
Marvin,
Arthur, and
S. Michael Gelber

O, it is excellent
To have a giant's strength; but it is tyrannous
To use it like a giant.

—Measure for Measure, ii, ii

PREFACE

BETWEEN the preservation of peace and the prevention of war there is a difference which, as the nineteen thirties indicated, may be more than verbal. Lacking a positive will to enforce the victory we had achieved in 1918, we were driven at long last from a negative rearguard action to the full sweep of 1945; the kind of supremacy we once enjoyed cannot be regained. The ignominy of the prewar decade, whatever errors in policy we again commit, may not soon recur. We have learned in a hard school that, while you can have power without freedom, you cannot have freedom without power—and that belief in your society is one of the foundations of its power.

Forewarned is forearmed. But now it is the very strength of its freedom that might cause an aroused, self-critical democracy to conceal nothing so much from itself as its own underlying strength. Within a dictatorship, at once leather-lunged and close-mouthed, total concealment is, on the other hand, a mute confession of an inward weakness. For as between East and West, the comparative position of the West may still, putting all together, be better than we suppose. And even our anxieties, by keeping us alert, can in themselves be a source of strength.

Such, at any rate, is the conviction out of which this book has grown. To weigh man's fate *sub specie aeternitatis* may be given to few. But over the years we can at least try to see major issues steadily and see them whole. And if these pages contribute a little toward that end, they will have served their purpose.

Some of the book's details, with the swift march of events, are bound to change. The forces at work, the broader trends, are unlikely in the near future to alter.

LIONEL GELBER

New York

CONTENTS

1

PERPETUAL CRISIS

The Contest of Power

WAR AND PEACE HAVE THEIR SYMBOLS, YET OVER international affairs as a whole there is neither presiding divinity nor patron saint. If, however, one were nominated, it should not be Cassandra, with her prophecies of doom, nor Dr. Pangloss, who thought all was for the best in the best of all possible worlds, but some robust offspring of the two. Upon the triumph of our arms a better order, as the reward of sacrifice, was promised the common man during the war. Victorious, yet disheartened, he now might wonder whether his exertions were not in vain; whether it was worth his while to save a civilization which, in an age of atomic or hydrogen bombs, may soon consist of little more than dead bones and broken shards in a silent, ray-laden or plague-infested wilderness. A more sober view of human prospects would not have raised wartime hopes too high nor allowed peacetime fears to plunge too low. For while on such terrain no road is safe or easy to build, one which neither winds to the clouds nor falls to the depths can yet bring us, along a middle route, to our destination.

Tomorrow's cynicism is the spoiled child of today's illusions. In the amelioration of the human lot all of us have the most vital of stakes; war distracts and diverts us from that preoccupation even where it does not demolish and debase. Step by step humanity must endeavor to go forward. Yet it cannot leap. In old Vienna it used to be said that the situation was desperate but not serious; in the postwar world the position may be serious without being desperate. For it is curious how extremes of pessimism and optimism meet when hot gospelers cry that all is lost unless their oversanguine panaceas are adopted; who by foretelling the worst if their solutions are rejected, show themselves up as men of little faith; whose failure of nerve thus singles them out as poor champions of the progress they espouse. Counsels of despair must not cause us to despair of prudent counsels. For when realism blends with idealism, it is freedom which is served.

Current disquietude is not only international in origin. Nothing has been more characteristic of the modern temper than the pursuit of what in daily life is deemed to be security. To North Americans, nurtured in a school of self-reliance and individual initiative, this mood—and the social legislation which it embodied—came late. Shared by all generations, it especially pervades a younger one for whom the frontiers of past opportunity have closed. Shoved into one corner by economic depression, flung by war into a second, they dread another turn of the same cycle before they have barely caught their breath.

Across the Atlantic the search for security, whether by reform or revolution, began during the late nineteenth and early twentieth centuries as a social and domestic movement. It took the turmoil of world war to make it international; to prove that if the well-being of individuals and classes is interdependent, so is that of countries and continents; to demonstrate that security at home may be in peril as long as it can be menaced by insecurity abroad. Between security in its national and international aspects the interaction is profound. Yet it is also evident that the one, even if it did not accentuate the political rather than the social, would be no mere extension of the other. Workable schemes of domestic security can be set up in some of the richer, less heterogeneous or backward countries. Disparities not only between each of them but between them and undeveloped nations would alone suffice to render any such all-inclusive project in the sphere of war and peace much more intractable.

Another distinction may be drawn. At its best a national security system might raise minimum living standards and protect the rudiments of a livelihood; with problems of life and labor which go beyond these, each person must grapple by himself. Politically, and in any world context, we are still far from that stage of security; internationally, the problems each country faces bear most resemblance to those of life and labor which its own citizens confront, not collectively, but as individuals. Security may, as a matter of fact, be practicable within nations to a degree which is impracticable between them. Yet over most of the earth even that initial objective is distant. Everywhere between man and man, between man and his environment the struggle for existence persists; on each level of society, in both private and public affairs, there is a ceaseless and multifarious contest of power. Even where contained by law and custom within a ring that is national, and not therefore so unmanageable, these processes and pressures are unsubdued; less should be expected from the rivalry of nations as single entities within a larger arena. It is, at any rate, a sign of maturity when we learn to cope with the fluctuations of fortune which life affords, to watch tides which ebb and flow. It may be a sign of immaturity in the attitude of many toward the question of world security when they seek, not to navigate acrid and tumultuous seas, but to drift across sheltered waters invariably placid and ineffably sweet.

An earlier conception was one of an order of law between states similar to that established within them. Yet this analogy also has, like that between social and world security, always been more plausible than practicable. If there were less absolute sovereignty in international affairs, there would, no doubt, be more of the world security which is our desideratum. Nevertheless, the draftsmen of the League of Nations and of the United Nations could not provide for the abolition of sovereignty; it is most improbable that the newer institution can in our day, by its own unaided efforts, drastically revise a principle on which it itself is founded. Yet we have scarcely staggered back to our feet after defending common interests and common liberties from one danger, before we have been compelled to band together in the common defense again. For international law to give security it would have to be universally enforceable through the world organization; instead, a balance of power is preserving it and the peace as well. Not that anybody can rejoice at recourse to supplementary yet traditional methods; but no critic has indicated how, by neglecting them and plumping for ideal solutions, we shall remain free in the crisis which impends.

Human nature is like the weather, about which, as Mark Twain said, everybody talks and nobody does anything. The race of man is not, of course, unable to change; and since our combative instincts might be deflected into nonlethal channels, there are within us no foreordained impulses to war. But there is a gulf to be spanned between the inertia of humanity and the pace with which, to save itself from obliteration, it is exhorted in the middle of the twentieth century to advance. International affairs are at least as intricate as national or domestic ones; political behavior in the former will not be more selfless or more intelligent than in the latter. For measures rather than men have been stressed in these matters, as if measures may be detached from the flesh and blood which contrives and applies them. If men are to suit measures, measures must suit men. But the grave needs of the epoch and the cult of the machine in the machine age have combined to lay fresh emphasis on the notion that some human device can yet be fashioned by means of which the tranquillity of our harassed planet might be guaranteed safely, infallibly, and through general consent. Peace by power is, on the other hand, like life itself, a peace with risks:

> . . . for the world, which seems
> To lie before us like a land of dreams,
> So various, so beautiful, so new
> Hath really neither joy, nor love, nor light,
> Nor certitude, nor peace, nor help for pain;
> And we are here as on a darkling plain
> Swept with confused alarms of struggle and flight,
> Where ignorant armies clash by night.

There is, alas, no formula of security which can work automatically, none which will replace vigilance, prescience, and judgment. War, after all, did not assail us in 1939 because for two decades we had lacked the ingenuity, the means, or the instrumentalities to prevent it. Even the League of Nations collapsed through no fault of its own; the setting in which it was designed to function, and perhaps over the years acquire authority, we ourselves vitiated or with gargantuan folly let slowly be destroyed before our eyes. The restoration of the European balance of power was the chief recompense of the victors for what they had gone through from 1914 to 1918; on that basis there was adequate security for the West, a foundation on which the League of Nations—though hamstrung in the Far East by American isolationism—could start to operate. To conserve that balance of power, as a matter of paramount self-interest, was child's play in comparison with what we have since been compelled to do. Yet the government in London which proposed that Italy be penalized under the Covenant for treaty-breaking in Ethiopia was the one which shattered the Versailles front by signing a naval agreement with Hitler. The Germans who had reintroduced conscription with scarcely a rebuke could smash the Continent's operational unity when they reoccupied the Rhineland. Vienna led to Munich, Munich to Prague; and when at last Warsaw was bombed, it was the peoples of the West who had themselves undone with one hand what they did with the other.

If, then, the world's plight is worse today than it was thirty years ago, we have only ourselves to blame. And if we wish to prevail now without conflict, it may not be through mechanisms of peace more ideally articulated than any we again possess. We cannot, when the stairs themselves are moving, retrace our steps. But unless we recall how we went wrong after 1919, we may still imagine that by the mere ritual of pouring old wine into new bottles the wine itself is chemically altered.

If the West had been less reluctant to admit that the war of 1939–1945 was, at rock bottom, a war for power—to wrest power from the Axis, to put it in the hands of the free—it might now exhibit less dismay at the necessities of peace by power. To preserve victory against former enemies and thereby maintain peace, to maintain peace against former allies and thereby preserve victory—the crisis of the twentieth century is a perpetual one. In many quarters there is, however, more understanding than there was a decade ago that a balance of power may not be premeditated by Machiavellian statesmen as a deliberate, one-sided plot against the liberties of others; that it has, in fact, been the response by some or many to a challenge of hegemony by one or a few such as Philip of Spain, Louis XIV, Napoleon, William II, or Hitler; that it is not the lever of a wider tyranny but an indispensable corrective against it. And to that extent a revolution in the thinking of the West about international affairs has occurred. We are less disposed than we were to hide the fundamentals of our freedom from ourselves.

During the war those who clamored most against its power implications were the ones who insisted that its prime significance was a social-revolutionary one. Yet social revolution as a consequence of war could do even its supposed beneficiaries more harm than good. The 1917 Revolution in Russia was long overdue. But among a people so ill prepared for representative democracy, the passage from constitutional reform to Communist dictatorship and world intrigue furnished Fascist propaganda, Nazi pan-German barbarity, and self-seeking reaction everywhere with a semblance of ideological cogency; in its fourth decade the Soviet Union appears, not as the emancipator of the masses, but as threatening or imposing a worse enslavement. This war has, however, been followed by moderate or nonviolent social revolutions in the principal democracies of western Europe. Yet against the revolutionary encroachment of Russian power their national independence and their own social and economic experiments are shielded by a still vaster revolution in another realm. For the most far-reaching change of the era is political rather than social; it is what the eighteenth century might have described as a diplomatic revolution—one which entails no mere exchange of provinces between princes nor any expedient recasting of alliances but all that and the bases of civilization itself.

The redistribution of power which marks our epoch is twofold in character. First of all, the balance of power in Europe has changed; in the second place, a completely new balance of world power is being formed. The war against Hitler signalized a second and belated endeavor by the Anglo-French grouping to dispute with Germany the domination of Europe; successful in the company of others, its victory was within an ace of being a Pyrrhic one. The Axis Powers may have lost, but France herself had to be liberated; while Britain, with the help of the English-speaking peoples overseas, barely managed to scrape through; on the Continent only Russia won. The East, having unloosed a struggle for mastery between Europe's West and Center, was itself to emerge on top. So far as it ever could constitute a rough, many-sided equality of force, Europe's ancient balance of power has been thrown out of gear or put into abeyance. Yet, in accordance with the most historic of rules, the assertion of an arbitrary, overweening hegemony must call into existence against it an even weightier preponderance. For the balance of power is not, as is usually believed, a single confrontation of forces approximating each other's strength, a scale poised thereby perilously in suspense. It is more analogous to a surplus, a balance deposited in a banking account on which the more solvent of competitors may draw to sustain primacy. And if tyranny again piles up a surplus of power in one area, the free peoples are able, as always, to outbid it elsewhere only by assembling a bigger one.

For as still greater strength is mustered, even the strong may desist. Against a fresh domination of Europe or Eurasia which, unopposed, might absorb all the continents of the earth, a global coalition is taking shape. Though new in leadership and broader in scope than any peacetime predecessor, the preponderance of the West will not differ intrinsically from earlier common ventures in self-preservation. Through the utmost in diplomatic pressure, by war only as a grim last resort, the free peoples must reaffirm their joint capacity to resist or never submit. And while there will be variations as rival strength rises and falls, no exact or near equipoise with it should be hazarded. A slender margin might encourage aggressors to try their luck; against an initial superiority or comparative equality an ultimate superiority in odds must therefore be stacked. Yet as the preponderance of the West is stiffened inwardly, the main fission of world politics will be narrowed. For when the foreshadowings of collective security under the wing of the United Nations Charter leave the weak a prey to the strong, freedom is mocked. A preponderance which protects and enlarges the frontiers of liberty may, however, by preserving freedom for the weak and peace for all, do more than anything else to inaugurate an ever widening reign of law.

And that, too, is why preponderance by the West would not be the same as domination by the East. For while the temper of the one is negative, preventive, defensive, that of the other is positive, militant, expansive. A dictatorship with satellite regimes but few willing allies, the Soviet Union would be dictatorial in its sway; voluntary in their combine, the Western peoples unite to uphold liberty, not to suppress it. The tradition of freedom in the civilized West is the inner check on its own ascendancy; it is the absolutism of the East which is at once intolerant and, if it spreads unduly, intolerable. Not that the West's own tradition of freedom has been as manifest as it ought to have been, either in the Occident or, above all, in the relations of the Occident with the Orient. Yet the tenderness displayed by it after two world wars toward mortal foes might suggest that in its preponderance there can be too dull as well as too keen a sense of domination. If, in the end, we fortify peace by power, it is because at long last—and better late than never—we recognize that contest for survival from which there is no abstention by the West short of surrender and no participation other than preeminence.

The new phase in world politics would no doubt be less disenchanting if we had first rid ourselves of the old one, if there could have been a settlement with former enemy countries punctuated by a recuperative interval before we were again immersed in a state of crisis. But as the pulse of events beats on, even an age of transition is no more than a period of time between one age of transition and another. The liquidation of the war was bound to determine the nature of the peace; Asia's chronic anarchy and Europe's momentous transposition of power were at once heirs of the past and progenitors of the future. For the future is no stranger who arrives unrelated, unannounced and, springing like Minerva from the head of Jupiter, fully grown; either in embryo or travail it is always with us. Yet because of that, rather than in spite of that, we should never abandon hope. The future may be less turbulent if with an eye to its antecedents our guidance is firm and no false upbringing lets it run amok.

To prevent the contest of power from degenerating into a conflict of arms is the prime business of statecraft. And though a spectacular emergency may shed light on the undulations of pressure, peace is seldom at the mercy of an incident. The sinking of the Russian fleet by Japan in 1904, the attacks in 1914 by Austria on Serbia and by Germany on Belgium, the German invasions of Poland in 1939 and of western Europe in 1940, and Hitler's onslaught on Russia in 1941 and the Japanese assault in the same year on Pearl Harbor were not perpetrated on the spur of the moment but according to plan. Nor were aggressors gambling wholly in the dark when they twice set in motion against themselves the fatefully interlocked machinery of counteracting alliances, friendships, and national interests. What they miscalculated was not so much their own attainment of victory as our acceptance of defeat. They would never have taken a chance had they foreseen not only the amplitude of our power, but how soon and how effectually it could be brought to bear. What they did was neither fortuitous nor spontaneous.

Between neighboring peoples all the world over friction is a commonplace. It is when such discord is aggravated deliberately and officially that serious trouble may ensue. A boundary dispute between British Guiana and Venezuela in 1896 and another over Alaska between Canada and the United States in 1902–1903 might have catapulted the English-speaking peoples into fratricidal slaughter. But as Anglo-American interests were converging and not diverging— the Anglo-American factor, which took shape in those years, becoming the foremost achievement of twentieth century diplomacy— their fiercest quarrels were soon turned to good rather than bad account. For in international affairs it is not the short-run incident but the long-run interest which decides. And while within the

West that long-run interest has been a pacific one it has with others often been bellicose. After the assassination of the Archduke Francis Ferdinand at Sarajevo in June, 1914, the policy-makers of Vienna, backed to the hilt by Potsdam and Berlin, resolved to exploit the outrage so as to crush the unruly Serbs once and for all; yet against the Anglo-French Entente in Morocco, Imperial Germany had long been fomenting and withdrawing from ominous incidents. At that juncture, however, her grouping was more likely to be the predominant one in Europe. Under the military timetable, from which neither alignment could then escape, it might subsequently be too late to strike with success.

After World War I, as before it, the hostile incident was again secondary to other considerations. Each major defiance by Hirohito, Mussolini, and Hitler of the Versailles and Geneva, Washington and Paris treaty system called for a showdown. Instead, the aggrieved chancelleries backed and filled because they did not wish to convert any violation into one; only when their most profound interests could be neglected no longer, when there was no third choice between resistance or capitulation, did still another incident in a mortifying series become the occasion but not the cause of rupture. And since that war, too, there has been a further illustration, in the Soviet blockade of western Berlin, of how the most potentially explosive of episodes can be subordinated to other things. Here, or elsewhere, the die might have been cast irrevocably. The Berlin situation can provoke war only when the East or West estimates that its vital interests may be served in no other way.

And for us now, harrowed and baffled by interminable crisis, there is in all this two simple lessons. The first is that symptoms of the malady should not be confounded with the affliction itself. The second is that unless or until it pays one side or the other to throw the gauntlet down it will be withheld. For power is the servant of policy, not the master.

And though this reassures us, it must irk the Russians. For they dare not put their continental predominance to the test without at once bringing into play against them a newly gathering world balance. Europe's wars and diplomacy have, it is true, long been influenced by what went on in the Americas, in Africa, in eastern and southeastern Asia, in the Middle and Near East, just as the impact of its contentions has been heavy on them. The power issues of today may even be what they were twice before in this century; but the stage of the drama is larger and the chief protagonists are no longer the same. Germany, too, is more abased than she was after 1918; in Europe, however, the balance of power has not passed back to those of her European conquerors who had previously retrieved it from her. So enfeebled were Britain and France by the war of 1939, that against the recalcitrance of the Soviet Union they alone could not even enforce the sort of settlement with the twice-vanquished foe to which they are entitled. The brute fact is that there would be no equilibrium in Europe (it would have cast off the fetters of one domination only to be enchained by another) were it not for the wider preponderance of the West—one to which western Europe, while a most important segment, is now subsidiary. For little but it stands between non-Soviet Europe and that imperium of the East which Hitler might have discerned with envy but to whose decivilizing values a Charlemagne or a Napoleon would have been averse.

Those who reject the concept of a power balance, continental or intracontinental, have yet to demonstrate how else the liberties of Europe, and thus our own, could, among the urgencies of the hour, again be preserved. For timing is all. What, in other words, peace by preponderance means is that the broader world balance must determine the course of events, not ultimately, as extra-European factors have twice done before, but primarily, immediately, and in the first instance. By the same token it is the equilibrium of world power thereby created between East and West through which the United Nations—as distinguished from the lesser European balance on which the more restricted League of Nations reposed—can do its share to soften and universalize the rigors of the power system on which such an organization has had to rest. For what fundamentally has happened is that instead of the world power struggle being any longer an aspect of the European power struggle, the European power struggle has become an aspect of the world power struggle. Geographically and strategically, in its more far-flung dimensions and in its shifted scale of diplomatic priorities, the new contest, though still centered in Europe, transcends it. For rather than be revolutionized by Russia, world politics elsewhere are themselves undergoing the most epoch-making of revolutions.

2 :

A NEW APPEASEMENT

The German Makeweight

IF SO MUCH OF INTERNATIONAL RELATIONS HAS, during the twentieth century, remained an incessant trial of strength, it is Germany which, among major Powers, did most to precipitate them from a struggle of politics into one of arms. Her defeat in 1945 was too severe for her to become a primary factor again—if ever— as fast as she did after Versailles; more speedily and more ominously than many anticipated, the East-West rift might permit her to be a secondary factor which could yet help decide the world contest against us. After 1919 the Weimar republicans, though inept, seemed to behave as pacifically and as democratically as Germans with a Western orientation say they intend to do today. Yet under cover of what also was an enlightened constitution, the forces of revenge were sleeplessly at work to subvert it; to reverse the Allied victory on which it rested and by revising the verdict of war change places with us. There was no excuse for our not acting in self-defense out of the ample knowledge about them we possessed at the time. There will be even less if now, having been twice bitten, we are not thrice shy.

Education was the elixir. While war raged, the skeptics were told that, swiftly and magically, this need but be undertaken to transform the German mind. What few realized sufficiently was that, in their outlook upon Germans, some of the principal victors might prove nearly as ineducable as the vanquished. For German ultranationalism,

13

though discomfited, did not wither away; as after 1919, it is again merely biding its time. "What we Germans want today," confesses a former German diplomatist, "is National Socialism without Hitler." Nazism, in brief, was a good idea badly executed; the repeat performance, as the Nazi strategists themselves said of the imperial German warmakers, will be better. At heart Germans may not alter. Will we in our treatment of them? For "the mixture same as before" is bitter medicine from which administering physicians can succumb even as the patient is rejuvenated.

On the subject of Germany, as on that of world affairs in general, many of us are apt to believe in the efficacy of an abrupt metamorphosis in national aspirations. Ethically, such wishful thinking is not reprehensible; politically, it has been, and can again be, a menace. It can also be curiously selective—the same quarters which manifest a lenient attitude toward Germany and the Germans often disclosing a more instructed, less unguarded view of Russia and the Russians. For the theory of sudden change, of discontinuity in historical processes, is one that is mesmerized by lulls after the storm on the surface; a sense of continuity is, however, conscious not only of these but of a violent undertow and persisting currents beneath. Reason, which is assumed to have been withheld from Germans though not from us, can, it is felt, now also be brought home to them. A button is pressed, the past cut off, and, lo! a day of fresh, unclouded Teutonic virtue dawns.

But reason alone seldom prevails; and it would be wrong to expect too much from education even if the correct sort for the German people could be ascertained and even if nationalistic or Nazi-minded pedagogues could be excluded from the transmogrifying process. The Germans have long been among the most literate of Europeans; the compatriots of Kant and of that retarded democrat, Goethe, of Lessing and Heine, of Einstein and Thomas Mann, might, over the years, have lived in the spirit of a patrimony as civilized as any in the West. At this they scoffed. Generation after generation, deliberately and with every ounce of their formidable energies, they consecrated themselves to national self-adulation, tribal myth, the cult of the warrior. Unlike the Russians, they have, since the French Revolution, been not unfamiliar with the ideals and political heritage of Western freedom. When the test comes, and the opportunity for something cruder beckons, they revert invariably to type.

Are Germans incorrigible? The answer, as always, is for them and not us to give—one not of pledges at present but of performance in the future. For the West to absolve them of sins which are not acknowledged, much less repented, and to frame policy as if they had already turned over a new leaf may yet be for the military and civilian dead of two German wars to have died in vain. Hell hath no fury, the poet wrote, like a woman scorned. If we were less prone to spurn Clio, the Goddess of History, we might hear less from Mars—or Odin and Thor.

Here, as elsewhere, the clue is Russia. Moscow after 1945, and quite apart from the special situation in Berlin, made a mockery of any such cooperative four-Power administration of the German economy as the Potsdam Conference contemplated. This left the American, British, and French governments with no alternative but to rule their own zones of occupation as they saw fit. The question was what kind of rule they would consider and establish. For Germany as a whole the three Western governments have sought a looser federal state, and the Russians one that is more centralized—one into which they, or their German affiliates, might thus eventually get their claws. Yet even a unified West German State, though mildly decentralized on paper, must, by the bald fact of its reunited existence, be a ready-made crucible for the resurgent ferocities of an unprincipled, ultranationalistic Germanism.

What the Soviet Union does in its zone of Germany, though exceedingly important, matters less than what the three Western governments have done in theirs. More agricultural than industrial, the puppet German Democratic Republic is handicapped by Russian plunder and that economic segregation from the rest of the country which has been the consequence of Russia's own intransigence. The western segment of Germany, with its 46,000,000 Germans, contains, however, not only the bulk of the German population but their chief industrial areas and their main industrial resources. And now that the fires in its furnaces have been stoked again, its litter swept away, its unification accomplished, and its heavy industries lumbering ahead, we may wake up one fine morning to discover that much, if not all, of the former Reich has become betimes a major Power once more.

To expedite that result are occupation and recovery policies which shelve the dismantling of German factories, wipe out reparation payments to Allied governments, and impede the restitution of their property to victims of the Nazis. Heavy and producer-goods industries need their own expert helmsmen at the wheel; we are therefore letting go unpunished, or welcoming back to their posts, directors and financiers who can serve as proxies for magnates and cartels which twice subsidized, supplied and exploited German militarism. Parliamentary democracy, which was to revolutionize all that, may thus again merely provide a façade for a managerial counterrevolution—with Germany's traditional merchants of death as contemptuous as before of their highly placed dupes in the West and as resolved as ever to betray them.

From the days of Lend-Lease it was evident that the United States would also have to endow and set going Europe's postwar rehabilitation. By its fusion of altruism and self-interest the European Recovery Program is a munificent exercise in American realism. But in Germany, where Military Government and the Economic Cooperation Administration did not always see eye to eye, the course pursued has been one of short-term practicality and long-term unrealism. For victory itself can become a rout when, as between the wars, it is followed by another flight from perspective.

There is no question that a Germany which is economically revivified and more nearly self-supporting will be both a stimulus to the prosperity of Europe and a relief to the Treasury of the United States. But the American taxpayer does not only have his pocket with which to reckon; it may be more profitable in the long run for free and straitened Europeans, foregoing early benefits, to be less dependent than before on German trade and German industry. For if there has been a lapse of memory about Germany in Washington, London, or Frankfort it is because—though this is not admitted officially—a counterpoise against Russia is being erected. If the principal sectors of Germany have been reamalgamated, it is on the hypothesis that as a single unit they can set up with us that balance of power which they themselves have just demolished against us. But it is not only their *bona fides* which may be in doubt. The entire notion of a strictly continental equipoise is obsolete. And as far as one can be partially restored, the recrudescence of German power may not serve the West but recoil upon it.

Germany's resurgence will come in two stages. The first is one in which the West, possessing freedom of choice, decides what might be done with its German zones of occupation and in which it can ensure, with its armed forces on the spot, that whatever is done should be on the Western model. The second stage is one in which the Germans, having been enabled thereby to resume their own freedom of choice, do not choose to exert it in our favor.

We are passing through the first stage now. And we had scarcely entered it before western Germany, shorn of penalties incurred by recurrent German war guilt, began to be rebuilt as a buffer against the Soviet Union. One of the main causes of the last war, this inveterate misconception of her role could yet be our undoing in another. Prior to the Nazi tenure of office, it was our French covictors, whose unpopularity in English-speaking countries was matched by the rising popularity of Germans, against whom vanquished Germany was sponsored. Only later did the Right in Britain filch that policy from the Left and Center so that Hitler, until he was beyond recall, could ride forth in his shining new armor as some blameless St. George about to retrieve civilized society from the Soviet dragon. Pacifism, which pervaded the English-speaking world, is the procurement of peace at bargain rates; and this was a bellicose adaptation of it, a vicarious bellicosity, at the same cheap price. For having out smarted ourselves and been outsmarted then, the bill is an exorbitant one. But to persevere again in a similar miscalculation may be to invite utter ruin.

Nor does the record convey that we have merely to revamp the political institutions of Germany to be safe. Since their ill starred 1945 Conference at Potsdam, both the Russian and Western governments have been committed to the broad objective of a united all-German democracy. No such four-Power scheme has, however, been adopted, because East and West can agree on neither the form of union—the West offering the Bonn Constitution as its pattern—nor the nature of democracy. As a result the western Germans have not had to pit one side against the other in order to slough off the shackles of defeat; that is being done for them and at a pace much more rapid than after 1919. Nor would they be loath to accede to a democratic system when with it they might regain so vertiginously the maximum degree of national strength that, short of absolute independence, is attainable. And for the moment such democracy might be less unpalatable by contrast with the Soviet terror under which Germans live in Berlin and the Russian zone. But when Allied bayonets are no longer there to prop it up, its duration may be brief.

What misleads and bewilders is that with their art and their science Germans have not only been in the vanguard of humanity but for over a century have harbored among themselves a host of sincere democrats. Yet within the past decade multitudes of their countrymen took part in, or acquiesced in, that civilian decimation of civilian millions, that cold, bestial state policy of planned human butchery by what was virtually a conveyor-belt system, which most postwar Germans attempt either to justify or deny but seldom condemn. Nor can it be supposed that minorities—Hohenzollern or Nazi—could hold so huge a Central European population as the German in thrall for so long, could muster and fling to oblivion year after year armies so vast, if they did not mirror the essential and historic impulse of the majority.

Thousands of German democrats, impeccably Aryan by origin,

did, nevertheless, also die the death of martyrs when they opposed or disobeyed Hitler. Tens of thousands rotted away in the primordial misery of his concentration camps. Yet from 1848 until 1933 none of them were able to band together in a pertinacious struggle against their tyrant enemies within; during the Weimar period the putsches and conspiracies of reaction, even when suppressed by republican governments lest the pains and penalties of Versailles be visited upon them, were winked at, if not aided and abetted, by the courts, by the army, by the bureaucracy, by the barons of industry and finance. And these were elements that either fostered the Nazis or steered the Nazi bandwagon on which they had climbed. The escape of most of them from any rigorous de-Nazification and the acquittal, not so much of obscure war criminals like Ilse Koch, but of such outwardly respectable major architects of the foulest Teutonic infamy as Papen, Schacht and Schmitz of I. G. Farben, is not therefore a good augury. For to forget and forgive is a two-way street which Germans themselves have never frequented.

By adopting the ideology of the West, they may hope to shake themselves loose from our power. Eventually the mass of a people so destitute of civic responsibility might again find a less representative type of government more congenial to its servile, regimented mentality. During the nineteenth century, when parliamentary liberalism was making headway elsewhere, similar tendencies also cropped up among individual Germanic sovereignties. In 1848, when these were so much the vogue in Europe, Germans even staged a series of *opera bouffe* revolutions; their spokesmen met at Frankfort to contrive national union and constitutional reform. But Bismarck proclaimed his unified German Empire in 1871; and the more it was nationalized, Prussianized, and militarized, the more democratic notions receded. And they did the same when the Weimar Republic, which had arisen not from German aspirations for freedom but out of the liberal demands of the Western victors, capitulated to the centralizing and coordinating Hitler without having struck an effective blow on its own behalf. Yet in spite of this, German nationalism since 1945 has fared so well in western Germany, with Allied troops in occupation, that it is not hard to conjecture how much further it might go if they depart.

Right and Left ran, after all, true to form during the 1949 general elections to the first Parliament of the Bonn Republic. Their chorus of hate, drowning out mere party differences, against those in the West who have been as much benefactors as conquerors, presages that unanimity in evil from which a militant Germanism always derives its strength. Yet when we let Germans, on a national scale, so quickly repossess the democratic machinery with which they can again negate democracy, we ourselves resemble them in one fatal respect. For if Germans are unteachable in their attitude toward others, we seem to be unteachable in our attitude toward them.

Such, at any rate, were the reasons why from 1940, from the outset of the Hitler war in Europe, one repeatedly suggested that while no perfect solution of the German problem can be envisaged, its least bad treatment may be to disunify what Bismarck joined together. If a greater Reich as united by him has twice desolated Europe, the way to preserve peace may be to decentralize it, to dissolve Germany as far as possible into her historic component parts, to detach from her completely and permanently the all-devouring arsenal of the Ruhr and the Rhineland, to dislodge Berlin from its niche as a national capital. The object was for devastated Europe to protect itself rather than inflict on Germans the chastisement they deserved; economic recovery was therefore to be promoted and so was trade between ancient Germanic sovereignties, between them and other European states, provided they fulfilled the prime condition of genuine independence. For the military striking power of Germany as a single unit might, one argued, thus be impaired.

Would these arrangements withstand a subsequent movement toward an ultranationalistic, all-German reunion? They could hinder the Germans during critical years between East and West when as a single bloc they might put themselves up to auction. To guard against their reunification would be costly. It might cost less—and could be acted on more swiftly—than the exhausting vigilance imposed by the specter (even if, for the moment, it be democratic and pacific in guise) of a unified greater Germany. And if that approach was cogent while there was a chance of the victor Great Powers being in concert, it is more and not less so when they are at loggerheads.*

Although progressive opinion frowned upon them when first advocated during the war, the papers of Harry Hopkins, the memoirs of Cordell Hull, and the recollections of Edward Stettinius, Jr. indicate that such ideas were afterward to be pondered sympathetically behind the scenes on the topmost level. Generalissimo Stalin proposed the partition of Germany to Mr. Eden and then to Mr. Churchill in Moscow. The Anglo-American exchange of views, with the Russians in accord, began on March 15, 1943; at the Teheran Conference, eight months later, President Roosevelt himself proposed a division of Germany to Mr. Churchill and Marshal Stalin. It would seem, however, that during the protracted discussion of this topic which ensued over the war years, each one of the Big Three was in turn to blow hot and cold. The Treasury or so-called Morgenthau plan was not to be prepared until the Anglo-American conference at Quebec in September, 1944, and the desultory three-Power debate went on after the Roosevelt administration had discarded that particular document. At Yalta, in February, 1945, Marshal Stalin raised the issue of disunification; Messers Roosevelt and Churchill concurred that it should be included in the surrender terms for Germany which the foreign ministers were to draft. Three weeks after VE-day, while visiting Moscow as special emissary of President Truman, Harry Hopkins discovered Marshal Stalin to be laboring under the erroneous impression that Washington shared London's altered attitude of thumbs down on a divided Germany. In fact, the United States still regarded the question as an open one; and the Russian

---

* The present writer's 1940 pamphlet was followed by his 1942 book *Peace By Power* (New York, London, Toronto, Oxford University Press), pp. 31–35, 89–99, where the foregoing contentions were stated more fully.

leader said that he, too, despite a recent public address to the contrary, would keep an open mind on it.*

Between Yalta and the termination of the Potsdam Conference, with the death of Roosevelt and the fall of Churchill, others were taking over in London and Washington. The incipient East-West postwar crisis, which had just sped Hopkins to Moscow, was deepening relentlessly. The Potsdam Declaration of August, 1945—a compromise itself thus already compromised—ensued.

To it we owe the initial decision that Germany would not be redivided into separate Germanic sovereignties. From its breakdown flows the further Anglo-American decision to establish a West German State of which the Ruhr and Rhineland would remain a part. To implement that policy, moreover, economic recovery was accelerated in the western zones, and it was a recovery based not on the consumer-goods industries of all non-Soviet Germany but on those producer-goods industries through which the enslavement of Europe had been twice engineered.

The day on which we might rue these decisions can come sooner than we think. For while by our power diplomacy we have dissipated the early prospect of a unified all-German state on the Soviet model, we have, in our breakneck haste, nevertheless created circumstances which both German nationalism and Russian imperialism may still exploit. The engines having been set in motion, there might now be no turning back; but when the whirlwind is reaped we shall want to know why the wind was sown. From Lord D'Abernon to Neville Chamberlain, the British appeasers pursued an astigmatic policy which was wholly in accord with the suicidal temper of the country. The American people, though alarmed over the East-West crisis, have not in this postwar period been similarly obsessed about Germany

* Robert E. Sherwood, *Roosevelt and Hopkins* (New York, 1948), pp. 711–713, 782, 787, 797–798, 818–819, 832, 904. Cordell Hull, *Memoirs* (New York, 1948), Vol. II, pp. 1167, 1233–1234, 1265, 1287, 1602–1622; Edward R. Stettinius, Jr., *Roosevelt and the Russians* (New York, 1949), pp. 121–126, 135–139, 162–163, 169, 344. For the present writer's analysis of Teheran and his renewed advocacy of a divided Germany immediately after the undisclosed Teheran proposal of President Roosevelt, see Lionel Gelber, "With Power to Preserve the Peace," in the *Virginia Quarterly Review*, spring, 1944, pp. 187–190.

and Germans. Yet what is being done in their name and at their expense resembles what was then done. It has also been undertaken by public figures whose abilities are not those of insight or foresight, who, though men of experience, despise, in their statecraft, the experience of Man.

The dangers which lurk in the situation are for the moment hidden by the Allied controls which have been adopted. There is, for example, an International Authority for the Ruhr to which Belgium, France, Luxembourg, the Netherlands, the United Kingdom, the United States, and West Germany itself belong. But with so little unanimity about the revival of Germany among the governments of the West, voting within the Authority over production disputes may tend to lift rather than preserve controls—especially if Anglo-American trustees are recruited from the ever potent, ever pro-German international steel cartel. The Ruhr Authority's terms of reference extend, moreover, only to the allocation of coal, coke, and steel; chemicals, engineering, and scientific research will have to be supervised, if at all, by the Military Security Board which the Western Powers are to set going throughout the Federal German Republic.

But the problem is not only one of surveillance by the West nor of the knavery by which secretly rearming Germans can cheat it, as after 1919 they tricked the Interallied Commissions of Control. Still less is it a question—over which the British Socialist Government disagreed with the Americans and the French—of whether the ultimate ownership of Ruhr industry is to be public or private. A nationalized industry can also be nationalistic—more especially since, as democrats and as internationalists, the German trade-unions have always been so flaccid and so inane. As a matter of fact, the Social Democrats were the party which first railed, under the Occupation Statute, against Allied restrictions upon scientific research, that industrial adjunct of German military prowess; they are still inveighing against it, against the Ruhr Authority, and against the Military Security Board—against, that is, the machinery of control which maintains our victory and their defeat. So, too, at the Bonn constituent assembly it was the Marxian Socialists and Liberal Democrats who, with the backing of the British Labor Government, agitated so vehemently for a centralism exceeding that of the Weimar Republic—for the tool, that is, not only of socialization but of German autocracy, military power, and European conquest.

Perhaps if the Ruhr and Rhineland had been dissevered politically from the rest of the German body politic, a union of non-Soviet Germany or even a reunion of the eastern and western zones would be less hazardous. The internationalization of this area within the compass of a larger German sovereignty is a makeshift which cannot be worth much. For a Ruhr Authority, a Military Security Board, a Charter for the Allied High Commission, an Occupation Statute defining Allied prerogatives and the West German Government's own field of competence, must all fight a losing battle for control when we ourselves are refabricating and reintegrating the tangibles of German power within a single national organism. To say that any subsequent peace conference will be able to review these portentous issues is to utter the most reckless sophistry; by what we are doing now we will confront the future with an irrevocable *fait accompli.* It is not that an eventual peace treaty over Germany is simply being prejudiced; in every essential except that of protocol this is the settlement which counts. Even with occupation troops still there on the ground, the writ of the West must become more and more awkward to enforce. When they depart, any cumbrous network of statutes and boards, authorities and observers under a supreme Allied agency of the three High Commissioners will either silently fold up or be booted unceremoniously out by its derisive wards. For the right to resume full authority which the victors reserve to themselves may be tantamount to the right of locking barn doors after the horse has leisurely been stolen.

Little sleep may be lost over this in North America, where such regulative machinery is dismissed as a sop to our nervous, over-excitable European allies. But Germany's eastern neighbors, while dreaming of liberation from the yoke of Moscow, may be quite as frightened by her resurgence; as between an old Teutonic and a new Slavonic overlord, they will not be emboldened to rebel against the one if they must thereupon resubmit to the other. On purely economic no less than general political grounds, the Economic Cooperation Administration is critical of eastern European countries which develop heavy industries instead of specializing in the agricultural production to which they are deemed best suited. Yet as the German octopus revives under these same American auspices, autarchy will be the defensive response in all quarters which dread the pinch of its tentacles. Certainly we are under no obligation to soothe the ruffled susceptibilities of Germans themselves over our administrative interference in their Ruhr complex by converting, as has been suggested, similar European industrial areas such as those of the Saar, Lorraine, Belgium, and Luxembourg into public utility areas. Upper Silesia is out of reach, and in the others what the West has to protect itself against is not strength but weakness.

If the Ruhr were less active would its populace suffer? Surplus population might well have been transported to outlying corners of the earth where it could make a new life for itself rather than be sustained in its accustomed mode of life by a venture which may again harry the life of Europe. Our modern world was founded on the migration of individuals and peoples—voluntary and involuntary —and there is no reason why Germans, who have caused millions to wander, should not for the sake of peace be uprooted themselves.

Perhaps, at any rate, the coal of western Germany, instead of being used industrially at home, could have been shipped to France. The steel mills of Lorraine may be more uneconomic to manage than those of the Ruhr; in terms of peace and freedom the uneconomic is often the more politic. So, too, the expansion of steel plants in North America, as in western Europe, might best expedite the rearmament and reconstruction of the West. Even though the American industry fears oversaturation in a slump, oversaturation in American steel, despite its depressive effect, would be less improvident in the long run than to let the Ruhr again be the pivot on which the industry of Europe revolves. Nor is the rebuilding of German heavy industry going to relieve the British and American taxpayer even in the short run. German competition in steel, shipbuilding, and chemicals must handicap Britain and France in their export drives, in their herculean efforts to recover from German aggression. And how this fits in with the parallel attempt to strengthen the Atlantic Powers is a riddle for which the Anglo-American economic revivalists of Germany have not deigned to furnish the key. For in politics a straight line is seldom the shortest distance between two points, and what appears to be going in one direction may be traveling in another.

Territorially, if the eastern and western zones of Germany were reunited today, they would not include the full expanse which Bismarck unified. After the 1914 war Alsace-Lorraine was retroceded to the French, and they have also reannexed the Saar Basin economically—to the chagrin of Germans but not of the Saarlanders themselves. There have been other minor border rectifications. In western Germany the principle of disunification into independent German states has, however, been rejected; in eastern Germany that of dismemberment—large sections, Pomerania, Silesia, East Prussia, having been swallowed up by two foreign countries—has instead been adopted. Russia assigned to her Polish satellite a considerable slice of Germany's eastern marches, so that the Soviet Union itself might carve from Poland's eastern terrain some of its own distended frontiers. The Oder-Niesse lands are, besides, much more extensive than Poland could defend against an otherwise unified Reich without Russia's armed assistance. An obvious source of a united Germany's future irredentism, they are Poland's grievous hostage to fortune and a trump card Russia might play against the West as they each vie for the *beaux yeux* of a resurgent Germanism.

At the Bonn constituent assembly West German nationalists complained over the amount of devolution upon which the occupying Powers had agreed and threatened to veer at once toward Moscow. This they cannot do as long as their hands are tied and we do not quail before Teutonic bluff and bluster. Yet the more we cultivate German nationalism the more we predispose ourselves to court it. Time, nevertheless, has not woven German sovereignty, despite all that is said to the contrary, into a single texture which cannot be unraveled. In 1919 Bavarian separatism had been quelled but the sentiment lingered on; as late as the Yalta Conference in February, 1945, President Franklin Roosevelt had inquired hopefully whether there were any separatist movements in Bavaria or in any other part of the Reich.* To the annoyance of post-Rooseveltian Washington, there apparently still were. At Bonn itself, spokesmen for Schleswig and Bavaria championed a confederacy of states against a close Reich federation. In 1949 the Bavarian Chamber refused to ratify the Bonn Constitution. In the election to the first Parliament of the Federal German Republic, the Bavarian party emerged with a solid bloc of seventeen seats.

During formative postwar years Bavaria, which is in the American zone of occupation, could have been offered economic inducements, such as have gone into the German phase of the European Recovery Program, and been set up either as an autonomous republic or Wittelsbach monarchy. Other Germanic states might then have negotiated with us on the same terms or even remained united. For with the Ruhr and Rhineland powerhouse detached from German sovereignty and with Catholic Bavaria, the oldest and one of the largest of German states, resuming its historic independence and again inclining toward Austria, the redivision of Germany would have been accomplished. Willing acceptance is more than her American paymaster and his fellow policemen could expect; but only in that manner might Germans be exposed to fewer warlike temptations.

Without some permanent system of coercion no settlement of this sort may endure. But what one will? Duress in the thirties would have saved us from war in the forties. Western victors, if they are banking on an early withdrawal of their occupation forces, may be certain of one result: the more a West German State is politically reintegrated and industrially fortified, the more contumeliously it can treat the West which has been reforging it. In 1922, when the French entered the Ruhr to penalize Versailles treaty-breaking, there was nationalistic resistance and self-inflicted impoverishment through a deliberate inflation of a war-weakened currency, but no effectual

* Sherwood, *Roosevelt and Hopkins*, p. 862.

nation-wide xenophobia. Popular and primitive Nazi frenzies were mostly repressed until 1930, when, the last of the Allied garrisons having evacuated the Rhineland, the rearming Germans could really be on their own once more. The constraint which Germans apply, when they can, to others is the only treatment they understand when it is applied to them. In dealing with Germany, as with Russia, peace by power denotes—peace by power. In domestic and foreign policy alike, a firm grip on Germans by the West is the sole assurance of their rational behavior. In unifying and restoring their economy against the Soviet Union, we must take care lest we unify and restore it against ourselves.

Soon even the most obtuse member of the Kremlin's Politburo may perceive this. It is not, therefore, surprising that the Russians should propose a withdrawal from Germany, as from Korea, of occupation troops. To neutralize and demilitarize her four zones, ironclad guarantees would somehow have to be devised. Yet if such were feasible, if East and West, while wary of the Germans, could trust each other, they might also be able to agree about other vexed issues; there would then be no major postwar crisis at all. And if Germany thus ceased to be policed internationally, could American economic assistance still roll on—but now with not even a simulacrum of control?

The end of the occupation would remove the chief land barrier that exists to the assertion of the Soviet Union's military supremacy everywhere in Europe. For the Russians can retire behind their own frontiers or behind those of their Polish and Czechoslovak captive states; they would still have at hand all they require either to support their agents and partisans in the two halves of Germany, to reinforce any pro-Soviet East German militia of their own, or even to parade back, after the troops of the West have gone, and lord it over western as over eastern Europe. For the countries of western Europe, their vigor sapped by two German wars, cannot by themselves oppose a total Slavonic hegemony. American, British, and French troops stationed in western Germany do not counterbalance Russian power with European power; what they represent, though their number be scant, is the combined, the preponderant power of the Atlantic world as a whole. Once they are evacuated to the outer fringe of western Germany, to France, to England, to America, they could never return to their foothold in the heart of the Continent without a head-on collision with the Soviet Union. But if they stay where they are, this may never occur.

Might not a rearmed Germany lessen the need for a continuous transatlantic intervention to stabilize Europe's disequilibrium against Russia? The opposite is the case. From the ordeal of the twentieth century we ought to realize that a strong Germany is more likely to take up the cudgels against the West rather than for it. In her German policy the United States seems to be of two minds. Facing the West, she reassures friends and allies who fear German power that a reunion of western Germany based on its mines and furnaces, the factories and skill of a virile populace, is a step which is strictly economic in its connotation, one which for Europe's sake can be restricted to the province of economics alone. Facing the East, she nevertheless relies on the renovation of German power as a spearhead in the political struggle between Russia and the West.

One truth is evident. The proponents of a European recovery and defense program which hinges on the industrial revival of the major portion of a reunited Germany know perfectly well that, in the modern age, productive power and military power are inseparable; that to distinguish the one from the other is as vain as trying to square the circle; that when you have great economic strength, actual and potential, great military strength is at your disposal. As the power of western Germany therefore increases and as Anglo-American leading strings are commensurately self-attenuated, what estimate can be made—in the light of past conduct and in terms of future interests—of how she will employ that power? In the postwar epoch few questions are more crucial.

The danger there is not one of Soviet intimidation but the prospect that the unified, self-governing Federal German Republic may be persuaded to swing voluntarily into the Russian orbit. The eastern and western zones being thus rejoined, their ruined cities and disrupted economy might not be as strong as was the Nazi Reich. Germany, if so reunited, could still furnish Russia with a substantial increment of unearned power—a windfall which might incite the Soviet Union, holding the Eurasian balance of power, to make a supreme bid for the preponderance of world power. No longer a menace when she is divided or stands alone, western Germany, as restored by us, can sell herself to Russia and thus turn the scales from West to East. The gravest criticism of Anglo-American policy in Germany is not, therefore, that it is designed to confine Russia on the Elbe, but that it may backfire, play into her hands, and provide her with the one indispensable auxiliary of her further imperial expansion.

Nor can western Germany's reviving trade suffice as a specific bond between her and her cosponsors—not, at any rate, if eastern and western Europe resume commercial relations. As competitors they will go each his own way; economic objectives are, moreover, always subordinated in German practice to national and political ones. Even less conclusive is any argument that western Germany would cleave to the West rather than the East out of gratitude for favors received or out of a common affection for polities of freedom. The recent history of the German people is adduced, in sum and in its dire effect, to counsel us against risks again taken with them on grounds as dubious as these. Representative democracy has never flowered on that flinty, authoritarian soil; nor in their recrudescence may Germans do more than jeer at the United States and Britain for bringing it about. From Frederick II to Bismarck, from Hohenzollern ministers to the megalomaniac Nazi upstart, they have been consistent in duplicity before all else. Where now would they have obtained a delicacy of feeling which debarred Germans, after being again nourished by us, from biting once more the hand which feeds them?

In Berlin and throughout the Soviet zone, the occupying Russians have been giving the once-conquering Germans a taste of their own harsh medicine. This is all the more galling when it is administered by what they deem to be an inferior race. Born of an ancient German fear of Russian encroachment across the flat plains of a Continent mostly devoid of natural barriers, the ever smoldering hatred of Teutons for Slavs is thus rekindled and fanned to a fiercer flame. But from Richelieu to Hitler, antipathies of race or creed have often been outweighed in power politics by dictates of national interest which transcend myth, emotion, or ideology. For Russia might beguile a revived and unified West German State into her camp with a number of enticements over and beyond any which the Western victor governments can proffer. Its establishment she has combatted tooth and nail because she regards it, together with the entire European Recovery Program, as designed to halt the Sovietization of Europe. Failing through tactics of discord and the diplomacy of pressure to crush it when launched, she may succeed alternatively in buying it off. And the guns she would have spiked can instead be turned around—German power being enhanced as she augments her own.

Reunion between the eastern and western zones is the first of the rewards with which Russia might bribe Germans into an alignment with her. And her chances of doing this are improved as the East-West quarrel over an all-German settlement is prolonged. For while one outcome is that Russia hugs her own German zone to her, the Allied governments allow theirs to grow in strength and autonomy. Of their own volition eastern Germans cannot budge; western Germans are, however, being rendered increasingly capable of doing so. To the West the latter must adhere alone; toward the East they and their fellows might rally all together. Unity being cherished among Germans more than liberty, the one can become the means of attaining the other. The freedom which is forbidden Germans in the Russian and bestowed on them in the Allied zones may thus be no ordinary weapon of the West against the East but a boomerang.

And then, secondly, even though not at once, Russia might hand back to a reunited Germany all of those eastern German provinces, the Oder-Niesse lands, which the Soviet Union allotted after the war to Poland. For the moment the Kremlin may feel that it has allayed the apprehensions of the Poles by vowing that their western boundaries will be forever immutable. But eternity can yield to expediency when a Russo-German bargain is in the offing; meanwhile, Moscow might play cat-and-mouse with Poles and Germans alike. There has been no four-Power German peace treaty and no final consent from Washington or London to the transference of this disputed territory. By exporting coal from coal fields thus acquired, devastated Poland is financing her postwar rehabilitation. And to lose them would indicate that a Russo-German rapprochement had again been concocted at her expense; that the Poles were being robbed of compensation in annexed German territory for eastern Polish territory they had ceded, from the Curzon line onward, to Russia herself. But there would be no novelty in that, except that this time all of Poland is under Russia's heel. In the game of powerful neighbors Poland has long been a pawn—from the more decorous eighteenth century until the day when Molotov and Ribbentrop signed that Nazi-Soviet pact which started Hitler's war and which should have taken none of us by surprise.*

Nor should a now Sovietized East Prussia prove a stumbling block between Germans and Russians. Moscow will not surrender to German irredentism the port and Baltic coastline of that much-fought-over, strategically important territory. There is much, however, which Germans can only reacquire by Moscow's fiat. Not even over the East Prussian nursery of Prussian militarism are they going to boggle—not at the outset, anyway.

The rewelding of the four occupied zones and beyond, which the West began, the East may thus complete. And the opportunity of reasserting internationally their reintegrated national power would then become the third item with which the Russians might tantalize Germans—another prize, too, over which the West can be outbid. For any Russo-German deal must, in fact, constitute an alliance, offensive

---

* In *Peace By Power*, pp. 147–154, the present writer republished his *Fortnightly* (London) forecast of March 1, 1938 (a year and a half before the event, more than six months before Munich), that such a Russo-German agreement would be the outcome of policies then pursued in the West; one by which Poland would be sundered and Europe put at Germany's mercy if Austria, as happened within a few weeks, were allowed to fall and Czechoslovakia were thereby encircled.

rather than defensive, drawn up against the West. Prime Minister Stalin knew what he was doing when, in October, 1949, as the Soviet Union recognized the government of its East German satellite republic, he reminded all Germans everywhere of the potential world force which, when united, they with the Russians can still exert together. To Russia, as senior partner of this colossal intracontinental combine, would accrue a larger percentage of the spoils. But an active junior partnership in an expansionist enterprise is likelier than any sedate, law-abiding association with the West to confer on German ultranationalism its still-coveted place in the sun. And being no apprentice but the more cunning member of the firm, it could yet pull itself out of temporary embarrassments to wind up as managing director, if not as chairman of the board.

A Soviet maneuver which turned the tables on the rivals of the Kremlin in the West would be one of real advantage to both Germany and Russia. In an epoch when atomic energy, guided missiles, radar, and biological warfare may be science's latest contribution to military power, the Russians can benefit from German research aptitudes; German technology might do something to counteract the huge industrial inefficiencies by which the Russians are hobbled; the labor man power, raw materials, and general resources of the two countries could be pooled. Germany's heavy industry, moreover, may thereby not only get back its passkey to traditional markets in the Russian sphere of central and eastern Europe: there is the Far East to be Communized through industrialization, and for that the Rhine-Ruhr arsenal could supply China with what Russia herself cannot spare.

In East Asia the progress of Sino-Soviet power signifies, as we know, a considerable setback for Anglo-American world policies. The restoration of German heavy industry might be the means of rendering this setback permanent; and for that, in all deference to vociferating, hand-wringing legislators, to Germany's Anglo-American unifiers and blinkered economic revivalists, we should have only ourselves to thank. For the time being the West has the upper hand in the Federal German Republic. Nevertheless, now that its giant industries have been reanimated by us, East-West trade may enable it partially to make its own way when we cannot afford competition from it in other world markets. And here, too, the Soviet Union, though denied control of Germany through a totally unified and fully centralized state, may pursue the same political goal through more roundabout economic ties—while the economic distress of the Soviet zone in Germany and of Soviet satellites in eastern Europe is alleviated. For though it was visualized as an obstacle to Russian world aggrandizement, the rehabilitation of right-wing German business can become one of the prime levers of the Soviet's future advancement.

More obscurely, there is the popular blandishment of anti-Semitism with which the Soviet Union may evoke a sympathetic response from impenitent Germans. The czarist persecutions, which the Nazis were so horribly to outdo, have not recurred; safeguards in Russia for national minority groups as such still damp down the murderous folk trends of the urban mob and the rural mass. Yet Zionism is banned, Judaism subject to the disabilities of other religions, and toward the activities of Jews as individuals or as a community the atmosphere has chilled. Litvinov, the Russian statesman detested by German aggressors as the advocate of collective security and Soviet collaboration with the West, has never been summoned back to high office. So widespread a phobia as anti-Semitism was capitalized by the Nazis, before and after their military push, to ingratiate themselves with the peasant peoples of eastern Europe. Among Germans the Soviet Union, as it now presses back from east to west, could, in its psychological warfare, return the compliment.

Above all, an alliance with Russia would cover the rear of a united Germany and she might thus exploit once more her own central strategic position on the Continent of Europe. Nor is it consoling to reflect that since Russian and German collaboration terminated disastrously in 1941, it probably would do so again. They did not part company before their conjuncture had ignited the conflagration of 1939. Nor would Germany be as capable as she was under Hitler of waging by herself a war of revision, of conquest, or revenge; the

Russians would for the first time be in the driver's seat. And if there is one contingency more than another which might convert the East-West crisis into a global holocaust, it is one in which a resurgent Germany can swing her weight to Russia's side. To preserve their world preponderance, to prevent Europe and Asia being totally organized against them, the Atlantic Powers might want to retort at once. Hoist with its own petard may, at any rate, be the outcome of that disencumbering German process which the West itself has set in train.

Between Russia and Germany a rapprochement can, moreover, be achieved through agreement rather than violence. As long as our three zones are policed by occupation armies, no Russo-German espousals may be consummated. Yet if our troops are evacuated or comparatively weakened by the concurrent recrudescence of a large German state, neither invasion from the east nor subversion from within would be necessary to ensure so sensational a result. In western, as in eastern Germany, the Communists might well be the most disciplined of parties; and while they may be employed by Moscow to indoctrinate the populace, final German decisions are governed not by ideological affinities but by considerations of power. The re-industrialization and federal unification of West Germany might therefore reduce poverty, in which Communism can breed, only to produce the national strength in which German East-mindedness flourishes. For countries other than Germany are also racked by Communist infiltration and intrigue. What makes it unique is that the impetus toward a Soviet-German alliance has emanated in the past not so much from revolutionaries at the bottom as from conservatives—aristocrats, army officers, leading capitalists—on top, from the Right no less than the Left.

It was elements of that stripe—German Big Business and the General Staff of the Reichswehr—which, sulking behind a cloak of liberal institutions and under the torpid eye of German democratic politicians, promoted the policy of Rapallo. And the treaty which they signed there with the Soviet Union in 1922 they not only renewed in 1926—when Locarno was supposed to demonstrate that Germany's ungrudging destiny lay with the hatchet-burying West—but was renewed and never denounced by that most impassioned of anti-Communist ideologues, Adolf Hitler himself. Today they, or their economic mouthpieces, are being reinstated in West Germany's seats of the mighty. To the addle-pated joy of the West, they won a majority of places in the new German Republic's first election. As much as any of the Kremlin's local marionettes, these are the factions —in whose activities the Center and the Socialists may once more acquiesce—which will have to be watched. For it is from recovery's golden rope and unity's iron ladder that West Germans, the manacles of defeat being again cast off, may best jump into Moscow's waiting arms.

A Prussian tradition which harks back to Frederick the Great, the objective of a Russo-German alliance was refurbished for modern Germany by Bismarck himself. Less well known is the vain effort of William II to resurrect it; his belief in 1904–1905, to the dismay of Russia's French ally, that it would have the support of both St. Petersburg and Washington. Often overlooked also is the annulling effect when President Theodore Roosevelt repudiated any such idea. For the German Kaiser had tried to create with Czar Nicholas II a vast intracontinental combine against that further grouping of the Powers (Anglo-American friendship, the revised Anglo-Japanese Alliance, the Franco-British Entente, preliminary Anglo-Russian feelers) which, a decade before 1914, was tending to counter Austro-German presumption. When Theodore Roosevelt, at the end of the Russo-Japanese war, informed St. Petersburg and Paris that he had not been offended by the second Anglo-Japanese Alliance but had been consulted during its recent negotiation, the British and French were not only reassured: an American President had helped give the overweening Russo-German ambitions of William II their *coup de grâce.**

* For an account of the wooing of Czar Nicholas II by the Emperor William II and for the key role of President Theodore Roosevelt in terminating that blighted romance, see Lionel M. Gelber, *The Rise of Anglo-American Friendship* (London, New York, Oxford University Press, 1938), pp. 173–174, 214–215, 240–247.

Autocracy within a new League of Emperors might then have been a bond. Between their two countries Communism would subsequently be no bar. Bemusing the West ideologically so as to expedite the destruction of Europe's balance of power, Bolshevism's self-styled archadversary put military necessity above the clash of doctrine. For in 1939 the Ribbentrop-Molotov pact relieved Hitler of what Bismarck had always dreaded and of that on which William II, despite unrequited endeavors to reinsure himself with Russia, had in 1914 gambled strategically—a major war on two fronts. The Nazi conqueror of Poland, France, and the Low Countries would not smash eastward again until he deemed his domination of Europe, Germany's inveterate aim, to be impregnable; when, that is, war in the east was now likely to be as much a one-front war as the Soviet itself had allowed war to be in the west. The scratching of pens in the Kremlin had been as the shout in the mountain snows which releases the avalanche. And Germans of a later era will regret not Hitler's first step but his second; not how he took his enemies in detail but how, in assailing his own Soviet collaborator, he overreached himself and reestablished the groundwork for a two-front war. The dazzling recollection of continental mastery, which Russo-German agreement had previously vouchsafed, still points to that exigent formula of alliance which, encompassing the deliverance of Germany from the West, alone leads on to the joint armed supremacy of Eurasia, to world power shared and thereby invincible.

On questions such as these, popular understanding within the Atlantic community, despite our treaty signatures, still leaves much to be desired. The error of many western Europeans is to dismiss the East-West crisis as one in which they are involved less by interest than by geography; the fallacy to which even some North American internationalists are prone is that what happens in Germany concerns her immediate neighbors more than it does the rest of us. Canada in 1914 and 1939, the United States in 1917 and 1941, by intervening to redress the European balance preserved their own national security. So now, but contrariwise, western European countries to protect their independence must do what they can continentally to reinforce that wider preponderance of the West without which they would go under. For our European friends should be disabused of the notion that any conflict in which their cities may be consumed and their lands overrun might stem from what is alleged to be nothing more than a Soviet-American quarrel, a conflict between outsiders in which quintessentially they have no part. Isolationism and neutrality have not ceased to be the vogue on this side of the Atlantic only to become the *dernier cri* on the other. One World *is* the issue, that one world of freedom which cannot be theirs without us or ours, ultimately, without them.

But while we may be embroiled together, the countries of western Europe are the more vulnerable. Mutual assistance and mutual rearmament within the Atlantic fold are designed to deter an enemy first of all, to defeat him as a last resort. But western Europe's will to resist can scarcely be enlivened by Anglo-American policies in Central Europe which might add to his potential strength. The two principal English-speaking governments have alternately scolded and mollified France, the Low Countries, and Scandinavia as though the resurgence of beaten Germany were a phantom of outworn anxieties, an anachronism of the imagination over which they are unduly alarmed. And so, mediating between continental allies and a late enemy, we, in our cooler, avuncular Anglo-American wisdom, comfort our friends with the patronizing assurance that nothing will be done at their expense. What we in North America have not quite realized is that what we do in Germany is done not only at their expense but also, in terms of American world policy and Western preponderance, at our own. On the subject of Franco-German or Russo-German relations we cannot sit remotely in judgment; we ourselves are now too intimately enmeshed. And so, in the last analysis, it may not be the French or other western Europeans, but we who have been parochial over this, our own Anglo-American policymakers who as leaders of the West may not have assessed the problem in its full magnitude and true global proportions.

It is most readily in Europe that, for weal or woe, the scales of civilization might quiver and swerve, rise and fall. And that is why the

Atlantic Alliance, while regional in application, is a world vehicle in a world contest. To it the reconstruction of Germany is a parallel attempt, an important feature of the Anglo-American endeavor to reestablish a continental edifice of power. Yet since any portion of a European structure that is German will be built on terrain with an eastward rather than a westward slant, the second of these regional efforts must in effect cancel out the first. The circumstances in which we might find ourselves are not then the familiar ones of France against Germany or even of western Europe's Brussels Treaty system against either Germany or Russia. They are those rather of a Russo-German compact whose total domination of Europe would suffice to match the once preponderant and thus relatively diminished power of the West. To afford Germany the casting vote of the Continent is not to correct Europe's disequilibrium through a world equilibrium, but so to accentuate the disequilibrium of Europe as to impair our own world predominance. Exercising their grim and gratuitous franchise in favor of the Soviet, the Germans may again be the ones to bring a showdown nearer. For the East would not only be made thereby less amenable to pressure from the West. Across its broadened Russo-German horizon the roseate mirage of total victory may swell and lure on to calamity.

Since Napoleon there have been two major treaty settlements—that at Vienna in 1815 and that at Paris in 1919—when the victors seemed to have within their grasp a world which might be recast, reformed, and shaped anew. While a third settlement has been begun with our lesser Axis antagonists, no joint one is in sight with their German and Japanese mentors. Instead, what the East-West crisis has done has been to illustrate again that, over Germany, a triumph in the field is only half the battle. In Vienna's system of peace there was the leadership of Great Powers, a Concert of Europe against a hegemony by any one of their number. That was its merit. The error it committed emanated from the nature of their regimes. For this required that they repress two modern impulses so deep-seated as nationalism and liberalism—the longing of men to be with their own kin under the same flag and free from either foreign or domestic servitude. In the 1919 peacemaking, however, liberal democracy and national self-determination were uppermost; the League of Nations was an international blend of these two principles. But Italian, Japanese, and German chauvinism were to renounce at home, and so also abroad, any such ideological fusion as the 1919 synthesis of nationalism and democracy. Their defiance the West could have handled in Europe by maintaining that continental balance of power which was the main recompense of victory and the structural foundation of the 1919 settlement. But as the Paris concert of victor Great Powers broke down, the balance of power which they had amassed so dearly was dissipated. The vanquished Germans could now seek to tether those by whom they had thus been untethered, and the war was resumed.

The peace of Vienna, despite its suppression of popular impulses, lasted a century. The 1919 settlement, though it catered to those impulses, expired ingloriously within twenty years. Between the two the discrepancy in their duration is astonishing. The Vienna settlement had started to crumble almost at once; from 1815 to 1914 every big conflict was, nevertheless, hedged in and localized. For one thing no Power, until the turn of the century, would challenge British primacy on the seas; for another, as the Crimean War demonstrated, not even Russia, her chief world rival during most of the period, wished to overthrow the European order on which Britain's world stature reposed. But in 1871, Prussia's defeat of Austria and France was capped by Bismarck's proclamation of the German Empire. If, for so long an interval, there had been no continental or general war, it may be because for nearly six decades after Vienna a greater militaristic Germany had not been hammered out of the independent German states; because there was no semiabsolutist Reich which, as Prussia writ large, would try henceforth and unceasingly to stretch beyond its own boundaries once it had unified itself politically and industrially between them. Until the Russian Revolution of 1917 it had been normal enough for Russia to join in the affairs of Europe. What finally unbalanced Europe's distribution of power was the impact on it of a greater, united Germany whose own sham democracy could always be subordinated to expansionist, Pan-German, ultranationalistic goals elsewhere.

Versailles, more than Vienna, contained within itself the seeds of its own dissolution. If the United States had ratified and if Britain had sought no loophole in their 1919 guarantees to France, it might have endured. But not if there were participation without intelligence. For while isolationism is nonparticipation without intelligence, appeasement may be to lack intelligence and yet participate. What we should now do, if we have rejected those twin phenomena of Anglo-American recreancy, is correlate the participationist stimuli of our own era with an intelligence derived from the experience of other eras. At all events, when the peacemaking of Paris enabled a greater Germany to hang on to most of the territorial, strategic, and industrial resources out of which are forged the weapons of conquest, it composed its own epitaph. The disintegration of the Austro-Hungarian Empire, the ostensible aloofness of Communist Russia, a drastic shrinkage in the ramshackle domains of the Turks confronted Europe with the most far-reaching of changes. But chief among the differences which had supervened on the Continent to distinguish the problem of Versailles from the problem of Vienna was the advent of a unitary German state, violent in discipline and disciplined for violence, as a Great Power. And when, against its dynamism, none afterward were to uphold the 1919 balance, all security vanished. For beside the ultranationalism of a unified Germany the national liberties of Europe could not dwell unmolested. One or the other had to go.

Today a renationalized Germany might be no more than a Teutonic tail on a Slavonic kite. Yet in becoming one it can shake off such constrictions as Allied policy and Western order would still impose; and tomorrow—who knows?—a successful Russo-German kite may be redesigned. The settlement of Vienna, while conscious of the realities of power, stultified itself when it repudiated the idea of progress. The epoch of Versailles, while imbued with ideas of progress, rushed on to its own demise when it later ignored the realities of power. Power with progress must, in any third major settlement, be the objective of the West. But it, too, will fail unless we perceive that more power for Germany means less progress for us.

In contributing to a German restoration, two normally opposed schools of thought have, as after 1919, tended again to chime together. The first of these is that of those who inhabit a serene, uncomplicated universe of their own; one that believes in freedom but demurs at the never ending struggle by which it is defended; and one which presupposes that you can ensure the reciprocation of good will by manifesting it. The second is that of those who, aware of the actualities of power, would nevertheless misapply them. For it is their postulate that in the mansion of peace there are doors to the productivity of Germany and to the stability of Europe which may be pried open simultaneously. What some latter-day realists and many genuine idealists reject is the notion of the lesser evil; that here, as in other walks of life, perfect solutions are improbable; that what we might manage is not the banishment of crisis but its abatement, its slowing down, its canalization between dikes which the diplomacy of power can alone erect. For the experience of a century may prove that German strength and general security are not so much complementary as antithetical; that you can have German unrest and a wider stability or German stability and wider unrest, but not the one without the other. And if that is so, the German Federal Republic will not add to Europe's balance but to its further imbalance.

The ramparts of the West, even if economic recovery were retarded and further material sacrifice entailed, should have been built behind its established frontiers. Statesmanship is the art of putting prudence before productivity and safety before efficiency. Europe is still bleeding from two German wars fed by the mines and fired by the furnaces and factories of the Ruhr and the Rhineland. Sundered irrevocably from western Germany, they could have been merged, if feasible and desirable, with French and other near-by industries; kept under the exclusive jurisdiction of the Western Powers, they might have been removed from the scope of any eventual Soviet-German agreement—if their severance from the Reich did not forestall such an accord entirely. In the European Recovery Program stress should have been laid not on rehabilitating the chief industrial areas of Germany but on expanding those of her western neighbors. Nor would this be for us to turn back the clock; it is Germany herself who once too often has done that. The mainspring of any improved European timepiece should, however, not be German in metal or design. It may be written in the stars that Europe can live only by a maximum industrial exploitation of a unified Germany's coal and iron deposits. But if that is the case, it may likewise be foreordained that a society at once so inventive and yet so trammeled by a dour, rigid, politico-geologic fate deserves nothing better than to be buried by them.

Should Europe, as an alternative, resign itself to a lowered standard of living? Such is to be expected, in any event, after what has occurred, with its human waste, obliteration of capital, decrease of intra-European trade, derangement of currencies, and loss of oversea investments. Until 1914 Europe could set before itself constantly rising criteria of material progress; when for a moment during the mid-twenties it seemed again on the mend, it may even have fancied that it might emulate North American standards. But the havoc of two wars and the toll of the postwar cleavage between the Soviet and ourselves are economic handicaps under which the overseas countries of the West do not have to labor in so immediate a fashion. For us to accelerate recovery activities which alleviate these is one thing; it is another if, while obstructing a Russian hurricane, we ourselves cause skies to darken which have scarcely had time to clear. Confidence is vital to economic well-being; security is psychological no less than military. It is good to raise living standards; it is better to preserve liberty in peace. While higher living standards may be the economic consequence of our German policies, the political consequence for free peoples may be to live without international standards or, in the sense of national independence, not to live at all.

Nor should we be misled by the theory, which served German interests so well before 1939, that a prosperous Germany means a pacific one, that if it were not for economic distress there would never have been a Nazi war mentality. From Frederick the Great to Bismarck no such compulsions goaded Prussia on to conquest; and it is in her spirit that the German national tradition is steeped. As a matter of fact, it was precisely the mounting world prosperity that imperial Germany enjoyed after being unified and industrialized which whetted her greed for more and more power. And it was as the outcome of this that the 1914 war was to be a Germanic line which, on the graph of European civilization, divided its formerly upward curves from those which have ever since been plunging downward.

Nor did the Nazi impostors get their backing from impoverished masses when despair, battening on defeat and on the inflationary devices of their own war and postwar governments, might have caused them to relapse after 1918 into the most barbaric of native Teutonic doctrines. In those early days of Allied victory their party enrollment was small. But they were to be supported at critical junctures by bankers and industrialists, by officers and aristocrats who hoped that a Third Reich would earn for them the world domination they had almost obtained under the Second—well heeled men of the Right who, while their underlings fought Communism in the streets, were themselves conspiring against the West with Moscow. The Nazis made headway, it may be remembered, only after Allied military occupation ceased—earlier than Versailles stipulated—and after reparations from Germany had been surpassed by unrepaid Anglo-American investments in Germany; after Germany, having thus been equipped by us with installations and machinery more up to date than that of her benefactors, could devote these to less undissembled rearmament on land, at sea, and in the air. Nor is it inapposite to recall in this respect, as in others, that, as she now competes in foreign markets or clandestinely rearms, her plant may again be new or, unlike that of the Allied victors, relieved of heavy capital obligations.

When, moreover, the Weimar Republic expired, the Germans were not the only people in the throes of economic depression—the late aftermath, in their case, of their own 1914 war and the strain to which they themselves had thus subjected their own economy. But none in the West had their maleficent faculty of combining Stone Age habits with twentieth century techniques—that final and characteristic expression of German ultranationalism which is Nazism. Franklin Roosevelt and Adolf Hitler took office not only during the same winter but at a time of severe economic adversity in both of their countries. The contrast between them, what they did and what, with popular assent, they each stood for, is the measure of the gulf which should be fixed between peoples who may, and peoples who may not, be entrusted with that economic strength by which power is generated.

How, then, is economic chaos within Germany itself to be averted? Our first duty is to her victims and our Allies. To bring the peoples of Europe again under the shadow of Germany may be the misguided continental phase of an otherwise correct world policy of counterpoise against Russia; to do this because Germans have in themselves any prior or special claim on our benevolence or good will is the chronic dementia of a society self-doomed by its own inversion of moral values. For to "organize sympathy" and soften up the West, to wage psychological prewarfare and drive a wedge between France and the English-speaking countries, were tactics of bedevilment pursued by Germany after 1918 so as to snatch back the victory which had nearly been hers. The drill sergeant's bark is what Germans respect. Fair but stern Allied directives, whether of political division or military occupation, might therefore have done as much as any reviving affluence to fend off mass Communism; to dispel the possibility of a Russo-German agreement they would have done more. From Germany, at all events, it is with prosperity rather than penury, as it is with unity rather than decentralization, that the Moscow road is paved.

The self-engendered misery of the German people could nevertheless be a menace, not only to their own physical health, but to that of Europe and of Allied occupation troops. Even in their contumacy they would have to be provided with assistance in foodstuffs and other goods. But expenditure of that sort, while onerous, must pale in comparison with the bill we shall have to pay when, with their political and industrial unification, they get a freer hand. Meanwhile, they have not done all that they should to grow their own food-stuffs, nor carry out land reforms so that inadequate holdings could be improved and Germans expelled from the east be resettled. The British people, though victorious, have, since the war, had to resort to the most intensive cultivation of their more limited island soil and the most equitable rationing of its products; there is no reason why the farmers of vanquished, yet now derationed, Western Germany should still refrain from doing their utmost for their fellow towns-folk. Incentives may be lacking; if Germans do not help each other, we ought not to help them. Nor have they only their own bootstraps with which to pull themselves up or our ever too vibrant heartstrings upon which they can pluck. Handicrafts and lighter urban industries could employ millions of Germans. A host of others might be job-less to the end of their days or barely eke out the most frugal of livelihoods. As a national entity they have nobody but themselves to blame if, after so pitilessly creating Europe's wretched problem of displaced persons, many of them themselves should henceforth have to languish in that dismal category.

Their numbers might have shrunk, moreover, as the good behavior of Germans gradually dispelled the just fears of neighboring coun-tries. Having been a treasonous, disruptive fifth column elsewhere in Europe, millions of pro-Nazi Volksdeutsch were dumped, after the war, back into an ungrateful and brutally inhospitable German lap. Yet Germans of the Swiss Republic have demonstrated that a Germanic community with a background that is neither militarist nor centralist can be loyal to others and might live democratically when the community is small. A firm Allied policy would not only have stifled the old nationalistic superciliousness at Frankfort and Bonn but rewarded trends toward disunification. For the more independent of each other the historic German states became, the more the West might have encouraged their separate economic viabilities within a broader framework of European rather than Germanic recovery. Since political unity and heavy industry as the epicenters of past prosperity and future revival should have been soft-pedaled, the aim could not be a standard of living such as Germany enjoyed before 1914 or to which, for an interval, she aspired between her own two wars. But the peoples of eastern and southeastern Europe have not starved with a simpler kind of economy. Germany and Germans, shorn for the world's sake of their delusions of grandeur, should have been forbidden anything else.

So drastic a process of readjustment would no doubt be both painful and protracted. But Germans have caused upheavals as vast for others; they may do so again unless they at last are the ones who have to give way. Many contend that, unless restored fully rather than partially, derelict and bombed-out Germany will remain a wrecked and squalid slum; yet even that would be better than for Europe to become a Teuto-Slavonic shambles. The West may feel that over against the East it is filling in Germany a vacuum of weakness; but a noxious vacuum which we ourselves have to keep distastefully half-filled may be preferred to a German solid which can be wholly inimical. For appearances are deceiving, and it is the paradox of power that against Russia the West is strongest when Germany is weak.

The abominations wrought by Germany and her sons are beyond atonement. What should have been pursued was no peace of retribution but one of self-defense; a settlement through which we would neither avenge ourselves on her nor she, as a single industrial-military colossus, ever be capable—alone or in alliance—of again avenging herself on us. Despite practical men, who on the major issues of society are frequently so impractical, there *is* a moral consideration here. But while forgiveness is a virtue, self-destruction is not; and before you can turn the other cheek, you must lift your head from the executioner's block.

The Federal German Republic may be admitted by its Benelux neighbors into their economic combine so that its competitive position can be, for them at least, a regulated rather than an unregulated one. There is also the recovery agreement between it and the Economic Cooperation Administration, as well as its entry into the

Organization for European Economic Cooperation. But, self-excluded by the German record from the Atlantic community, it can have no arms; and without arms it may not belong to the Atlantic Alliance or the Brussels Treaty. By a clause in its constitution the unified West German State might, however, join the Council of Europe. Yet it would be anomalous to admit as an equal member a German republic which is restricted by Allied controls, not only of her internal economy, but of her foreign relations. Out of zeal to include her in the wider body, such controls themselves may tend to become dead letters. Nevertheless, it would be safer to admit the German republic as a semisovereign member into the Council of Europe than for all European countries to shed their sovereignty and merge with it in a tightly integrated federation of western Europe. For this would not protect Europe from the military resurgence of a reindustrialized Germany. A people as ill trained in democracy as any large, united segment of Germans could scarcely participate with free non-German peoples, some of whose own democratic institutions have not been devoid of strain, without jeopardizing the entire project. Striving to dominate it, they might coalesce with other Teutonic racial elements throughout Europe and try to wean the polyglot federation away from the West, or smother it entirely. Nor are the French, as we establish an Allied supreme council, likely to forget an old danger while also combining with us against a new one.

Much ingenuity has gone into the making of our German policy. The rudiments of the situation are as crude and bleak as ever. For no amount of dexterity will allow us to reconstruct a major portion of the industrial strength of a federally reunited Germany without putting within her grasp an elaborate, eventually uncontrollable, war potential. Against the West the defeated Germans can now no longer go their own way alone; together with the Russians they might, quite literally, find new worlds to conquer. What the question may then boil down to is one of Germany's revival or Europe's survival. Through any indiscriminate effort to restore the European balance with German help, the world preponderance of the West may be lost.

3

AN ARMED TRUCE

The East-West Schism

IF THE HUMAN QUALITIES NEEDED TO ACHIEVE victory were the same as those required to conserve it, we should neither have allowed World War II to occur nor be harassed by the problems it was bound to leave in its wake. Coalitions may dissolve, not only because a common cause has vanished, but also because, when the enemy is no longer at the door, to retain what has been gained calls for the sort of insight which the mass emotions and herculean exertions of war do not normally elicit. The task of preservation at a time when forward-looking ideals for postwar society have been fostered is apt, moreover, to be regarded as a conservative one. Yet nothing in the 1930's did as much to muddy the waters as the betrayal by the moderate Right of this, its natural stabilizing role. For throughout that decade of ignominy none in the West manifested a radicalism more violent than most Conservative leaders, other than the Churchill wing, in their self-defeating approbation of those vengeful revolutionary forces which, behind the counterrevolutionary cloaks of Fascism and Nazism, undermined the 1919 settlement, erased a victory purchased at so terrible a cost, and shattered irretrievably an order of European power which withstood the assaults of 1914–1918, which Versailles renewed and which the victory of 1945 could not again adequately restore.

When dragon's teeth are sown, no harvest of daffodils is reaped. And when ideological sympathies are not subordinated to the national interest, foreign policy must always be out of joint. Yet a conflict of ideologies may exacerbate mistakes without creating them. The setting for our 1939 war was furnished twenty years before, when the United States rattled back into an isolation from which even the Washington treaties did not wrest her; when Britain and France began to cross swords in Europe and the Near East; when the great Bolshevist Mother was mainly intent upon devouring her own revolutionary children. The 1919 coalition dissolved, not on ideological grounds, but through the noncooperation of countries whose principles of politics and whose way of life was one and the same.

As then, so now—the concert of victor Great Powers which emerged battered, yet triumphant, in 1945 might have fallen apart even if ideological rivalries did not aggravate their dissensions. For changes of the most fundamental character had been set in train. In their second war with a Germanic grouping, the Anglo-French combination was again on the winning side; but of the two principal victors one is European only in a peripheral sense, and the other is not European at all. And just as the identity of the chief actors has altered, so has the scope of the play. Always the main center of world politics, Europe is now no more than one of its most important sectors. The crisis we are passing through is therefore a crisis of adaptation—one in which the new protagonists, while taking each other's measure, are also assessing their own larger part on a larger world stage.

Unlike the prewar situation, and though we differ over elements of policy, our side is clear about the nature of the struggle in which we are engaged. And that gives an air of reality to the contest of power which is in itself a long step toward peace; we had to know what it was about before we could do anything about it. Ideological inroads might have carried some free countries of the West into the Soviet camp; none, it is noteworthy, submits voluntarily when American economic aid is forthcoming and Russian bayonets are kept at a distance. For even so potent an ideology as Russia's needs power behind it, if it would stride magisterially ahead; when the path is barred by equal or superior power, it too must call a halt. American forces of occupation in Germany, together with those of Britain and France, are few in number; but for one simple fact they could either be trampled over or driven back into the sea. That simple fact has, however, been decisive. As tokens of the full amplitude of American-Atlantic power, they will be defied by Russia only when she can venture on a total showdown; and of this not many signs can be observed. For there has been a general post on a global scale. No European balance exists which, with indirect American support, could stave off the Soviet Union. At work instead is the whole new world balance held mainly and directly by the United States—but one in which the former custodians of Europe's balance, being thus bolstered up, may more and more also take part.

Less strange than the revenges brought by the whirligig of time is the soil on which it spins. For as Russian imperialism has again pushed forward in eastern Europe, in the Balkans at the Dardanelles, in the Middle East and eastern Asia, it is not so much an Iron Curtain that descends as the curtain of history that is raised; even Alaska has a familiar ring, and as a minor scene in the air-age drama only the North Pole may be new. It is quite another feature of the plot that is profoundly novel. For a century, and until the Triple Entente was formed on the eve of World War I, Russia's main rival was the British Empire. Today the hand is still often the hand of Britain, but the voice speaks English with an American accent. In Iran they have stood together; but in Greece it is chiefly the United States which, under the Truman Doctrine, has been implementing a military-economic policy, inherited from Downing Street, to save the eastern Mediterranean from Soviet penetration. And when Washington, with money and arms, backs Turkey against Russia, the spirit of Disraeli himself seems to hover over the Potomac.

Revolutionary chaos at home, threats from one quarter or another in the Occident or the Orient, at first gave the Soviet Union's expansionist pressures a tentative air. But with the collapse of Hitler's Germany and of imperial Japan, they could again be set going full blast; and from cold storage to cold war was but a step. Strategically estopped in the West, Russia has nevertheless seldom been internationally more secure. To rectify frontiers, to seek friendly states on her borders, to obtain warm-water ports were legitimate aims which had the assent of her Western covictors. But she went far beyond them when she cowed and Communized neighboring countries and attempted to subvert more distant ones. The bases with which she is surrounded, projects of economic recovery, continental unity, and Atlantic defense were summoned into being by herself and against herself as she did all she could, short of war, to ensure her own arbitrary domination of postwar Europe. After her defeat by Japan in 1905, Russia, while licking her wounds in East Asia, again concentrated on the Balkans; and this in turn threw her against the Austro-German bid for European hegemony, with the war of 1914 as the result. Now, however, she has no peer in Europe and but one elsewhere. From Central Europe to her still extending Asian extremities, she is able, as long as she does not overstep the mark, to operate more freely than ever before.

But what is the mark she may not overstep? It is one that would bring into play against her the over-all preponderance of the West. Where, at the outer reaches of her self-aggrandizement in the Orient, that point might be located cannot be foreseen; in Europe proper there is less room for speculation. Western governments, whatever intermediate fatuities they may again commit, could never allow Russia, even with the consent and assistance of Germans themselves, to combine a united Germany's strength with her own—to form a Eurasian bloc not only with a tremendous war potential but with a military stranglehold on the whole of Europe. For while this might not shift the world balance entirely from one pole to the other, it would produce between East and West a state of parity—one in which there was no longer a preponderance of power to make aggression a risk which dare not be taken. From the Russian point of view, however, a pact between a revived Germany and the Soviet Union should be by agreement rather than subjugation; sabotage of an imposed Soviet rule would reduce the strategic usufruct of so prodigious a venture. But no voluntary agreement will be easy, despite Communist disaffection, pro-Soviet intrigue on the German Left, or a military-industrial compact on the German Right, if our occupation policies are firm, our occupation troops alert, and our Atlantic Allies rearmed. Nor could bounds be set to such an agreement. For the Russians, once they start, must try to overrun Europe to the Atlantic. And it would not pay them to subdue or hold the capitals of western Europe as ransom for the safety from air or even air-atomic attack of their own cities and industrial agglomerations. Russian power will have gained little and lost much if it devastates western Europe only to have the inner citadels of its own national strength obliterated.

As for the defense of North America, the same new dimensions in world politics apply. Ocean barriers and frozen wastelands have not evaporated. Our more numerous centres of power might by themselves be more vulnerable than Russia's from the air; our world-wide political relationships must also furnish our greater strategic air-power with more widespread outposts for retaliation. No Russian invasion to blot out the forward bases of the Atlantic Allies in Western Europe would thus be worth the counter-chastisement summarily inflicted from all directions on the heart of Russia herself. And atomic or hydrogen weapons, as with poison gas during 1939–45, may for that reason never be used. Fear of reprisals should prevail in the East as much as in the West—if not more, then not less.

To great land power, at any rate, there are earlier limits than to a long-range air power with which is coupled predominant, global Anglo-American sea power. Overextension would apply an inner brake even if Russia functioned with the efficiency of her rivals in the West. But she does not. Germany, when unified and centralized, is a military danger—apart from the strategic value of her geographic situation—because the Germans, being as well schooled technically as they are docile politically, can always bring their maximum weight to bear as a single unit. In alliance and by sheer bulk the Soviet Union, as distinguished from czarist Russia, may have overwhelmed them. But with a still unlettered peasant mass, and with a bureaucracy so administratively poor in an economy of bureaucrats, the more her monolithic system expands, the more it must sag under its elephantine load.

War from the air would not, of course, eliminate the task of land forces to follow through, to mop up, and to occupy enemy domains. For that traditional purpose, Russia, where life is cheap and where an enormous human reservoir is scattered outside urban targets, is less handicapped militarily than others. But on land, as in the air and at sea, war nowadays is more one of machines than of men; the competition of power begins in the factory and the workshop long before there is the arbitrament of battle. And here it is the modern technician—the man so much more typical of the West than of the East—who must eventually carry the day.

If the Soviet Union overreaches itself, the physical stamina of the Russian people will be of scant avail. As a continental land power, it has specialized in the production of heavier tanks and bigger guns than the United States, but its oil reserves are smaller; in steel—that telltale gauge of industrial power—motor cars, and machine tools its capacity is less than western Europe's and only a fraction of North America's. The Russians may have ascertained how to make the atomic bomb, but without knowing its latest secrets or without having comparable resources to spare for the process of manufacture or to overtake the American stockpile; and now there may be an even more deadly hydrogen or triton bomb. In the design of self-propelled missiles, German experience is being tapped by all parties. Russia's jet, fighter, and other tactical aircraft may be more numerous than that of Britain, the United States, and Western countries; these can be outgunned by long-range American strategic aircraft which might not only be atom-armed but might, in a pinch, serve from home bases. In railways and mobile transport—the key to supply in land operations and to governance in any durable conquest —the Russians are deficient. The test, however, is not a statistical comparison of what weapons each side now possesses; it is whether, no quick victory having been obtained, one side or the other is paramount when its productive potential is actualized to the utmost. Millions of Soviet ground troops were never demobilized after the

war; huge tracts of Russia, again ravaged by the Germans, have had
to be reconstructed; while undertaking another one of her Five-Year
Plans she must satisfy the pent-up demand of a long straitened populace for consumer goods. And if the armaments race in which she
has nevertheless engaged becomes one of beggar-my-neighbor, the
burden rests not only on North American capitalism and Western
democracy, whose downfall she has anticipated with such naïveté,
but on social progress within the Soviet Union even more. For the
price of trying to do too much is to do nothing really well.

Not that the West is uninhibited in maneuver. A totalitarian dictatorship, having dragooned its own subjects and having warped the
public mind, may unloose an offensive without warning them or the
foe. In the West neither the conscience nor the social outlook of its
peoples would permit a preventive war; as the American and other
democracies deliberate, time can be spent which allows an enemy of
the Atlantic Alliance to get in a paralyzing initial blow. Yet unless
such a blow is decisive everywhere, the net military advantage would
be ours. Nor is that due only to the prior possession of the atomic
bomb and the greater strategic capacity to deliver it, but to a system
of which these are no more than a crowning operational phase. That
pioneer of American participation, President Theodore Roosevelt,
as he intervened in a European crisis, shared in Anglo-Japanese
diplomacy, and mediated in Russo-Japanese peacemaking, was wont
to rate the staying power of democracies above the striking power
of autocracies. In the staying power of the West is the stuff of its
preponderance.

What, then, must shape the world contest are not only military
factors which happen to be palpable at the moment, but others which
are implicit rather than explicit—imponderables which both under-
lie and go beyond the current tug of contending ideologies. Even in
Europe the territories to which Russia's power has stretched are, by
the technological criteria of the West, relatively soft, backward areas
—or, at least, as in the case of Czechoslovakia, without a solid hinterland for resistance or support. Yet if the tide turns, many of them
might be not so much a defensive asset as a Soviet liability. Russia's

power must, at all events, thin out as it spreads. Between Russian and German aggression one difference, however, should be noted. Germany, in her two wars after Bismarck, was so situated geographically that when she expanded she came to grips at the outset with other major, developed Powers, or they with her; wherever her legions might march she had to conquer the West or be conquered. Russia, too, through war or subversion, may be bent on the conquest of the West. But while her mysteriousness is traditional, her traditions have been no mystery. In all major conflicts since the French Revolution —and the bungled interlude of the Crimean War was not one of these —Russia has ultimately been aligned with those who tried to restore Europe's balance against a single, voracious domination, against Napoleon Bonaparte, William II, and Adolf Hitler.

Does the Muscovite gamekeeper want to turn poacher now that Prusso-German power might be a brace rather than a menace and now that from the Asiatic mainland the ancillary danger of Japan has also been removed? The Revolution having been saved through Russia's traditional course in foreign policy, will the Kremlin, torn between revolution and tradition, decide that such a national tradition should itself at last be revolutionized? If it does, there will be a counteracting force not dissimilar from that to which Russia herself has hitherto belonged. For a revolutionized world strategy would invoke Europe's own past tradition as it unites the free world against what, of all steps taken by the heirs of the Russian Revolution, may fundamentally be their most revolutionary.

As contrasted with Powers which excel at sea or in the air, the Soviet Union, a jailer of other peoples, is the prisoner of her own inert, land-locked immobility. Despite radar and numerous interceptor craft, Russia's sprawling domains expose to attack a larger unbroken surface than do those of her adversaries; with close political ties binding the latter together, the United States is furnished with strategic steppingstones which give her better air access to Russian territory than Russia has to American.

Even in peacetime a serious diversion by Russia in the Middle or Far East might afford an opportunity for the West to redress the

European balance. Land power, on the other hand, is contiguous to victim nations; antagonists from the West would be compelled to move against Russia around the edge of a vast circumference. Britain learned that during their long nineteenth century duel; in our own day we have seen how Teutonic land power possessed interior lines which its enemies lacked. And what, in fact, most differentiates the postwar from the prewar power of Russia is the unimpeded command of these on a Eurasian scale. On the eve of 1914 Japan was kept from jumping again at her throat through their common association with the Entente. From 1939 to 1945 Russia was saved from a coordinated onslaught between the eastern and western sections of the Axis, first, by the Nazi-Soviet Pact and, second, after Pearl Harbor, because Japan was as eager to be master of the Orient as Germany was to be master of the Occident. With the Axis demolished, the threat has vanished of any inner Eurasian encirclement of Russia. But an outer world coalition is what on its own perimeter Soviet imperialism has provoked against itself.

Around the globe this is spearheaded by the strategic air power of the United States and the air-sea power of the United States and Britain. American aircraft can operate in the far Pacific area from Manila, Okinawa, the Japanese islands, Alaska; had they not been outflanked by Communist rule over China, there might even be East Asian footholds from which Russia's industrial region in the remote fastnesses of Soviet Central Asia would not be altogether secure. In the Middle East and along the Mediterranean there is a growing series of bases on which Anglo-American sea and air power can be centred. France and other of our Atlantic Allies are girding up their loins in western Europe; in Germany the West may be accoutred for more than occupation duties. Britain, moreover, is not only rebuilding her own land, sea, and air forces, but in the United Kingdom, to supplement the defense of the European continent, is stationed an American air-atomic group.

For here, all over again, is the historic strategy of the nutcracker. But now it has been magnified from continental to global proportions. By the use of her interior lines Germany endeavored to shatter first one and then the other jaw of the nutcracker she had been forging against herself. Unlike Russia's, however, her interior lines were planted on the outskirts, near the jugular veins, of western Europe; these, moreover, she could lay out and organize with facilities in transportation and a capacity in management which the Russians cannot emulate. For the German General Staff tried to offset the effect of war on two fronts, against which Bismarck toiled and into which William II and Adolf Hitler dragged them, by switching their forces backward and forward, by concentrating them on one side or the other for a maximum impact. Twice they almost pulled it off; twice they failed. Within Europe and Asia the Russian bloc is not ringed around as the Germans feared to be; but they have a more unwieldy expanse to protect and the new unfathomable dimension of the air in which to protect it. Because their interior lines are at once so extensive and so sparse, regional independence has been established in the Russian armed services and the Soviet war economy. But such decentralization may be incompatible with a totalitarian society and the technological resources of the Communist state. Less vulnerable to a multilateral air assault, it might be more of a prey to industrial and strategic bottlenecks.

Stress abroad will thus entail strain at home. Were it western Europe alone which she still had to face, were Russia concerned with but one continental land front, none there could stand up to her. On the European continent, however, it is not merely the isolated and inferior power of western Europe with which she must cope but the European branch of an encircling world system superior in power to her own; one by which western Europe is sustained and whose strength the renascent vitality of western Europe must in turn augment. The contingency of a single or coordinated attack on Russia by Germany and Japan has been replaced by that of multiple counterpressure from other and wider fronts. For whatever she may strive to do in the air or by submarine at sea, she is confined essentially to the one, all-absorbing, Eurasian element of the land. Satellite regimes might beat a path for her from eastern Europe to Malaya; the Russians, like the Germans, have always been less unwilling than we to make cannon fodder of their youth. Yet once the operational limits of intracontinental land power are touched, the mobility of the Soviet Union must peter out and that of the other side move ahead. The postwar crisis differs from earlier ones, not only in the range of weapons and the peril, should war ensue, in which they might put us all, but in having changed its main contestants and in an enlargement to planetary size of the power contest itself. It remains, at bottom, the same.

And such being the posture of affairs, has the conflict of ideologies no share in them? Its share is a considerable one. For what Russia dare not seek through open rupture she plans to accomplish by boring from within. An economic catastrophe in the West, which would gain her the revolutionary allegiance of its dispossessed, is a hope deferred but not an aim discarded; in foreign Communists, like their Nazi and Fascist counterparts, Russian imperialism has its political vanguard. Apart from these, however, some in the West will soon have persuaded themselves that what, during the past three or four decades, distinguished the democracies from the dictatorships was our outright opposition to totalitarian ideas. The legend may soothe many an eminent conscience; it is a legend nonetheless. So busy between the wars were exalted figures in preferring one set of totalitarian ideas to another, or in advocating neutrality when the common freedom was menaced, that all were trapped by their numbskull frivolity. It was by exploiting the ideological sympathies of those they gulled and undermined that our Nazi-Fascist enemies accumulated military power. Only in the nick of time did we learn that we had to master their power before we could dissipate their ideas; that although, contrary to them, we rejected power as an end we could not survive in their kind of world if we repudiated it wholly as a means.

It was, however, inevitable that one idea, the idea of nationalism, should work against the Nazi-Fascist power of its own accord. And against Russia's expansion the same old leaven must again slowly ferment. Through the interior lines of Eurasian geography, her power, and not the West's, has territorial access to China; the armed revolution there, which looks to her for guidance and must take help where it can get it, is in its most rudimentary stage. With her Chinese collaborators, Russia can promote her own imperialism in Asia by putting herself at the side of national movements which are shaking off the yoke of other imperialisms; in eastern Europe the erstwhile liberator of her smaller neighbors has replaced German domination with her own. As long as Russia's ties with the more distant peoples of Soviet or non-Soviet Asia stay loose, she can make good use of them. But in eastern Europe she has treated her own allies as if they were no more than semiautonomous members of the Union of Socialist Soviet Republics; they have cultural self-determination with few political or economic rights as nationalities or individuals. And that spells trouble.

For if she provokes unrest among captive nations and satellite armies, Russia cannot rely on them unreservedly and under any circumstances at a grave juncture between East and West. Communizing revolution accompanied the uprooting of Nazism and Fascism within the nonindustrialized countries of the Soviet sphere. Yet even there the break-up of large estates and the growth of individual peasant proprietorships may have created a vested interest in the destruction of feudalism—French Revolution, rural style—rather than in the reinstitution of despotism, in a doctrine the agrarian undertones of which are more liberal than Communist. Farm collectivization on a thoroughgoing Soviet model, together with its trade subservience to the Russian economy, may be attained in eastern Europe. Economic distress in that area, its need of East-West trade, illuminates, none the less, the shortcomings of Soviet policies of self-containment. Nor did Russia's own peasantry accept collectivization lying down. Tito himself may also insist upon it. Yet if it is achieved elsewhere, that will not be because the Kremlin's gospel is so puissant but because its armed power is so near.

The Communist rulers of Soviet Russia may only repeat the error of their czarist predecessors when they suppress or absorb foreign peoples for any purpose, ideological, imperialistic, defensive, aggressive, of their own. To establish a cordon of buffer states on her borders, provided it did not go beyond that point and as long as it might be harmonized with the interests of her neighbors, was, in the light of past events, an intelligible policy of national security. But their strategic value can, in the air age, be overrated; and in any case the dour political servility and cruel ideological conformity which the Soviet juggernaut wrings from them has been such as to thwart Russia's own objectives. Grateful for another liberation from Germanic trammels, her East-European allies may now become discontented, sullen, and furtive; helots waiting until a military defeat or diplomatic setback administered their oppressor elsewhere enables them also to rebel—until the power of their nationalism allows them to exercise a disruptive influence on Russia's national power.

Tito is the first such chink in the Kremlin's armor. And, like other heretics, he claims fidelity to a truer version of the Communist faith than Moscow's. Alone among the satellite revolutions of eastern Europe, Yugoslavia's was home-made; like Mao Tse-tung's regime in China, it owes much to Moscow in general but nothing to the Red Army in particular. And in estimating the relationship between ideological and diplomatic power, it is significant that Tito's independent national Bolshevism would germinate in a southwesterly country of the Russian sphere to which geographically the West has naval-military access.

Against the Cominform blockade of Yugoslavia, economic aid from the West may or may not dilute the orthodox purity of Titoist doctrine. But in the conflict of ideas, when Yugoslav nationalism takes priority over Russia's own expansive nationalism, it is as though a clarion call to others—one by which even the Kremlin's thick walls may be pierced—had sounded.

Elsewhere in eastern Europe there have been lesser but similar portents. In Bulgaria, however, deviationist personalities have been purged, and no more is heard of the proposed Balkan Federation. For while this latter could mitigate the nationalism of its members against each other, it might also permit them to assert in common and on Russia's southern flank a certain independence of her. More clear-cut are the bitter qualms of Polish and Czechoslovak patriots over renewed threats to their territorial integrity and Europe's peace when Russia, espousing German unity, shows herself disposed to sacrifice their vital defensive interests on the altar of her own world ambitions.

Within modern police states nationalist uprisings do not stand as much chance as they did in old-fashioned tyrannies. The heroism in the last war of the anti-German undergrounds was therefore all the more remarkable. During that, however, and because of all by which it may be so hideously disfigured, nationalism was condemned. But one argued then, as one argues now, that it is a force with which we cannot dispense if we wish an order which will be both international and free.*

For in the Occident, though not in the Orient, nationalism has long been depicted as innately retrograde. And, as among those who have debased religion through bigotry, some peoples have been corrupted by it; over the years it has galvanized others to strike for elementary liberties against a foreign yoke. What matters is how it manifests itself and by whom. German nationalism, being incompatible with everyone else's and having twice desolated Europe, should be curbed—as it cannot be when it has a reunified state within which to flourish; Russia's may be corroded by the effect on her totalitarian empire of those she has subjugated. For nationalism, like power or life itself, is either good or bad in accordance with the cause to which it is dedicated.

An itemized reckoning of war potentialities between East and West can therefore tell but half the story. For the light and flexible ties of the one may be tougher and more durable than the massive yet brittle power of the other. All who are with us are here of their own volition; among the nations of the Occident, if not of the Orient, whichever are with Russia have no opportunity of being anywhere else. If, as in the Napoleonic formula, the moral is to the material as nine to one, it is in the realm of the imponderables that the West's preponderance will ultimately be reinsured.

Do hydrogen and atomic bombs modify this evaluation of military

* *Peace By Power*, pp. 54–58.

tangibles and political intangibles? With these cataclysmic weapons either side might retaliate; as between East and West, the West's relative margin of general advantage is therefore retained. Our preponderance could no doubt be destroyed by a knockout-blow—by a surprise bombing, atomic or hydrogen, from aircraft, from submarines or from a nearby steamer, on the industrial and administrative nerve-centres of North America. But to dispel fear of a similarly annihilating attack in return, Russia must utterly wipe out, and at the same precise moment, every other major installation of counteracting air power all the world over. Nor can she spring an atomic-hydrogen onslaught on some of these first, or on the great capitals of Western Europe alone, without the highly dispersed machinery of Atlantic retribution leaping back on her from elsewhere. Geography must impose operational differences. In principle London and New York, Paris and Washington, Brussels and Montreal may be protected by one, connected, world-wide air strategy.

Not that the rulers of Russia are haunted, within the elastic confines of their Eurasian sphere, by the same dread spectre as ourselves. For they know that unless they themselves first unloose a global holocaust, nobody will. A license for audacity, it is this which enables them to capitalize on the moral and political restraints of the civilized West; it is this which affords them, despite the din of propaganda and the blare of doctrine, an unadmitted reassurance which they do not afford us. The trust they have that, short of a final showdown, we would not strike is thus at the root of a forward course fanned by what is ostensibly their distrust of us. In the long run the Russians, too, must proceed within the same bounds as ourselves and under the same terrifying menace.

If warmakers did not expect to escape from the horrors they inflict on others, there might have been fewer wars. And if in exterminating their rivals, they now cause themselves also to be exterminated, for what will they fight? Nor would Russia's exemption and the West's destruction serve the Soviet's own purposes—national or ideological. A Western society whose physical structure stands intact may still be Communized or Russified; but not even the Kremlin would have the macabre wizardry with which to resurrect it from radioactive rubble or hydrogen dust. Modern war, without either atomic or hydrogen bombs, is frightful enough. And though the Soviet Union seeks to redress the world balance, there are tacit limits, as long as we maintain our preponderance, beyond which it cannot venture. Wars to end wars having bequeathed us a peace to end peace, mankind is, like Mahomet's coffin, suspended in mid-air between earth and sky neither making peace nor waging war—denied the one but from the other reprieved.

Why, then, does Russia clutch this two-edged sword so tightly? Seldom in history would counterpressure on her have been so slight if, after 1945, she herself had relaxed her own outward pressure. Not that she is loath to change her tack when favoring winds blow more at one point of the compass than another—conferring with Powers while slamming doors on agreement, cutting her losses in Berlin or Greece while counting her gains in China, veering up and down a broad Eurasian surface but never altogether pulling in her sails or dropping anchor. And this hankering for storms out of which she rides but does not wholly eschew may emanate from the desperate inner logic of the dictatorial system itself. For only a perennial state of emergency could justify the continuing subjugation of even a people as ill tutored as the Russian to a tyranny that came to depose tyranny. The alarums and excursions of an expansionist policy thus serve, as in the days of czarist autocracy, to rivet on them the chains they have reforged for themselves. When the fatherland is surrounded by foes, real, imaginary, or self-engendered, the loyal sons of Russia can scarcely begrudge its rulers their abject and unquestioning obedience. And if pride of patriotism, as the nation's power grows, does not compensate for daily hardships, there is the short way, which every absolutism takes, with dissenters.

The free peoples of the West, during and since the war, have been urged to find a dynamic similar to that which has impelled the dictatorships. In principle there can be no quarrel with this. While refusing to curtail individual rights or muzzle representative institutions, we might thus attract to our side those who have neither political nor economic freedom or to whom political liberty without economic opportunity is a hollow shell. But revolutionary regimes, with their so-called "dynamics," are like the center of a vortex: only in the midst of interminable unrest do they induce an illusion of calm; only through a succession of crises is the inherently unstable furnished with a persisting semblance of stability. In *Alice in Wonderland* it was, after all, the *Red* Queen who had to keep running in order to stay where she was. There may have been foreign plots on Russian soil during the late thirties; the purges of that era, preceded by the wholesale liquidation of the kulaks, were savage even by the historic standards of Russian tyranny. And it might well be that world turmoil today fulfills the same purpose as the purges and liquidations of yesterday. The fatherland, when threatened abroad, must not only cling to its seasoned leaders, but the national interest also requires that it undertake the severest reprisals if at such a time —and it is, in one manner or another, always such a time—any would murmur against it.

That foreign and domestic exigencies are but obverse sides of the same medal, dictatorships understood sooner than democracies. Nor is it any wonder that, for a few years after the fall of the Axis, the Soviet Union should have been more of an adept at crisis politics than the United States. For the latter, while no novice in world affairs, has, until now, never known her own strength—much less tried, other than in war, to make the most of it. Communist ideologues have, on the other hand, always been trained to power concepts, the world contest being but the class struggle translated to the plane of diplomacy. And realism, the one peace-saving lesson which the pre-war Axis should have knocked into our own thick heads, but did not, we now have to display toward Russia as we learn it from her.

One observer, reminding us that force and fear are its ordinary instruments of domestic policy, suggests, moreover, that

to the Kremlin they do not seem as dangerous in foreign policy as they appear to the Western Powers. Rulers and people, perhaps rulers more than people, live in a political and moral climate all their own, and the postwar extension of Soviet power carries this strange atmosphere for the first time into the Western world. We have to inure ourselves to these blasts of Soviet-made weather. There's just a chance it may not be as threatening as it seems.*

Europe, it was said in the days of the Franco-Prussian war, had lost a mistress and gained a master. Now, however, it has lost a master and gained a committee. And while there may be day-to-day ignorance of the West in the Politburo, its general postwar obduracy might indicate a shrewd sense of the possible. By its own ethical principles and modern democratic processes, the West has been precluded from retorting in kind until a breaking point is reached. And because diffidence such as this is in itself an invitation to hostile pressure, power organized against it is a move not toward war but peace. Before 1914 few of the chancelleries would have tolerated a series of challenges such as the Soviet Union has flung into their teeth since 1945. In 1941 the invading Hitler risked everything against Russia upon less provocation. But against the West the Politburo has ascertained experimentally what it could get away with, how far it might go. And then, having pushed in that direction to the utmost, it may alter its tactic as another opening occurs or as the West itself now stiffens all down the line.

For in Soviet world policy it is a national rather than ideological interest which is supreme. *Raison d'état* is not only with us once more; it is one that in the eyes of Communists everywhere exalts the *status quo* which exists in Russia while they strive to overthrow the *status quo* outside her sphere. Pan-Russian rather than Pan-Slav, this morbid, self-regarding, revolutionary nationalism might have been changed in emphasis by the struggle for office which went on among the heirs of Lenin. In the long run, whatever the outcome, the effect would no doubt have been the same.

Behind the Russian lurks the Tatar and when the Communist is scratched the Russian will be found. Stalinists were for revolution first within Russia herself; Trotskyists averred that you must have

* Anne O'Hare McCormick in The New York *Times*, Oct. 9, 1948.

it there and concurrently throughout the world. On the procrustean theory of simultaneous world revolution, the more typically Marxian one, anathema was pronounced; it was the less inflexible of the two dogmas, with its accent on the national rather than the international, which won out. Rigidity in dialectic may have continued, but elasticity in its practical application had thus been blessed; the watchword from the Comintern to the Cominform might well have been: Trotsky is dead, Long live Trotsky. And there is no reason to suppose that, whatever may be the succession to Stalin, his success in expediency will be revised. For under him Communism has been a frigid yet variable fanaticism which invokes the ideology of world revolution—in the fulfillment of which Russia herself, as its all-powerful progenitor, would occupy the central niche—but may depart from it. Patriotism, which is abhorred by Communists everywhere else, is beatified in and for Russia. For this is the acme of *sacro egoismo*—the crusade that was to liberate mankind reduced to the narrowest *Realpolitik*, one which would overturn the world order lest by it Russia's socio-national revolution be overturned.

Yet such nationalism, not that of Russia's subject and satellite peoples but her own, can again rob the postwar crisis of its warlike sting. For with the Soviet's self-engrossed nationalization of Communist internationalism, this phase of the world struggle might also be compressed or have boundaries put around it. Given a local habitation and a name, treated in concrete terms of national interest which at each stage can be measured and may therefore be compromised, it should be less arduous to pin down than a clash of ideologies whose tenets, at once so fixed and yet so elusive, are universal, incommensurable, and uncompromising. Policy as framed by East and West may have as its ultimate objective the collapse of the other side's system of government. But in the air-atomic age, the Communist doctrine would not be worth much if Russia herself is flayed, gutted, and scourged. It is therefore a national interest to abate the monomania of ideology and accept the survival in the West of a mixed non-Communist economy, half-capitalist, half-socialist, until, as prophesied, this breaks down under its sheer inability to provide for the common man. For while a serious depression has not yet brought about the long-sought and world-wide revolution of Communist endeavor, it is better to wait and see, or to hasten that contingency by agitation and conspiracy, than to tempt Fate by war.

With Fascism and Nazism abased, though not eradicated, the ideological issue has been clarified. What the postwar crisis is now serving to demonstrate is that two systems, such as the Eastern one of revolution and the Western one of reform, can somehow co-exist. Yet the East-West cleavage, while also a contest of socio-economic ideas, is much more than that. The years from 1914 to 1918 and 1939 to 1945 were but recent examples of monarchies and republics, autocracies and democracies, single and multiparty regimes joining hands. And the national interests which overrode ideological differences sprang from a common stake in a world order larger than each. The issue of world order had to be settled against the Axis by war. The issue of world order can be settled against the Soviet bloc by peace.

But will it? If the power behind the East-West contestants were approximately equal, the answer could well be in the negative; if the Soviet rulers permitted themselves to be carried away by the ideological missionary fever they themselves have excited among their own people, they might have been disposed before this to underestimate the likelihood of defeat. But the power behind each of them was not equal in 1925 when the predominance of the non-Soviet world extracted a modification of Communist doctrine and it is not so even now. The West's potentialities, despite the armed might of the East, are still preponderant.

Nationalism, it is usually said, makes for war, while universalism makes for peace. By the experience of our epoch we may want to temper that lofty yet undiscriminating judgment. For as with power itself, much depends on which nationalist or universalist ideas are involved and by whom they are borne. But even if Russia had not been nationalizing the pristine universalism of her doctrine of revolution, it would still be the case that ideologies do not fight. All that they can do is facilitate or impede the struggle for power whose weapons in the world contest they have so patently become.

Events are the test. Totalitarian dictatorships have not, as has been claimed, sprung up in the wake of Byzantium rather than Rome; many of the Germanic lands were outside the orbit of either, while Fascism arose at the very *fons et origo* of Latin civilization. It is a fact, however, that despite the subsidized efforts of Communist parties abroad to subvert the free institutions of the West, Communism has only been set going in a corner of the earth whose ideological heritage is, like Russia's, authoritarian; or where, as in the example of Czechoslovakia, a nation has had to capitulate twice, not to foreign ideas, but to the overwhelming force mustered by their nearby exponents.

And if that is so of the Occident, it is no less so of the Orient. Representative democracy and civil liberties have been even more alien to its methods of government than they are to eastern Europe's. In Asia, however, revolutionary nationalism has had its guns trained, not on Russia's territorially connected empire, but on the scattered empires of the West. She accordingly champions it there while striving to efface it in her own European sphere of influence. Within the larger contest of world power, this is a conspicuous exhibition of the unprincipled use to which ideological principles can be put. But the Russians now, like the Japanese before them, would not be able to resort to it so brashly if, in the Orient, the democracies of the Occident had themselves been quicker to live up to their own principles. Yet the more distant Communism gets from its home base, the more it must adapt itself to other conditions; and the farther it stretches out in Asia from Russia's own long arm, the less recognizable it will be ideologically. In most of the Orient the process of imperial disintegration and national reintegration is incomplete; Russia, with her geographical proximity, could not avoid fishing in its troubled waters. Yet the West, once it gets its own house in order, is infinitely more capable than the Soviet Union of helping to raise what, in an exact Malthusian sense, is Asia's bare level of subsistence.

And if that were done, power economics can—as with wartime Lend-Lease, Greek-Turkish aid, the European Recovery Program, and the Truman proposals for the development of backward areas—again subserve power politics. For while the national interests of Russia might coincide with those of the Asiatic masses at this juncture, they can fork off from them later on. Awakening, like many in eastern Europe, to the fact that they have but exchanged one set of taskmasters for another, the peoples of Asia may lift their eyes to the West once more. Russia's burdens in organizing her own productive power are manifold; in any attempt to shoulder new ones elsewhere she might flounder and fail. Without the investment capital, the technology, and markets of the Occident, the raising of Asia's living standards may well be stultified. Nor would Russia herself necessarily derive profit from the economic modernization of an Asiatic satellite such as China. As the West has been doing in Germany, she may merely rear a Frankenstein there against herself. For while Germans can best retrieve their world position by consorting with Russia, to the Chinese she has always been inimical. If the Germans seek freedom of action, the Chinese must want action for freedom. And while the one may be attained by alliance with Russia, the other is to be achieved by an alignment against her.

To illimitable ideas there are no political limits. The expansion of Russian power can, however, be delimited by the amount of effectual power arrayed against it. And that, too, is why the narrower concept of a ceaseless struggle for power is a less tragic or pessimistic one than the notion of a war to the death between all-embracing ideologies. Diplomacy is credited more frequently with its losses than its gains; it may divulge least when it could disclose most because it might be a handicap in any future negotiation if we gloat now over those who have had to climb down. What, under a broad historical perspective, has peaceably been averted by the steady, unremitting exercise of preponderant power we only recall after anarchic interludes when, as between the two wars, we let power slip so maladroitly through our own fingers; we seldom remember the continuous dividends which for long uninterrupted periods did, and with competent stewardship might still, accrue. But the wisest diplomacy will be impotent to preserve peace or wage successful war if the power behind it is insufficient for the purpose.

Of any such standstill in world crisis, live and let live can be an unacknowledged ideological by-product. Reminiscent of an earlier situation, it is not exactly the same as when the peoples of Europe had to desist from their religious wars lest all be decimated and when, as swords were sheathed, the battle of theologies grew less fierce. East and West have growled and bared fangs at each other; as a practical measure of mutual safety in the air-atomic age, their virtual armistice must precede and not follow hostilities. Yet if the strength of the West were less, or not more, than the East's, no stalemate might occur. For it is not both, as in earlier ideological conflicts, but only the weaker of the two camps which has been on the move; and while each would suffer from war, it is not the West which alone needs peace. A doctrinal piping-down might be difficult for the side which, by the nature of its being, must thrash about ideologically more than it ever could politically. Those nations are preponderant, at any rate, in whom the liberal democratic tradition of tolerance—in itself an outgrowth of the wars of religion—is now ingrained. And it is precisely this ideological tradition of tolerance which makes tolerable the preponderance of the West. It is the lack of any such tradition which, outside its own sphere, would render so utterly intolerable the preponderance of the East.

Russia's own recent somersaults in foreign policy cast light on the subordination of doctrine to national interests. She herself was to pay the heaviest of penalties when, by signing the Nazi-Soviet Pact in 1939, and so banishing the historic German nightmare of a major war on two fronts, she let Europe burst into flames. But Moscow's betrayal of the Munich betrayers illustrated, at least, how Russia could sink antipathies between Communism and Nazism in what she conceived to be the exigencies of power. And two years later, when Russia's own independence was assailed by her 1939 confederate, when a contrary view of national interest thereupon ensued, East and West hushed yet another set of ideological differences and stood together against the same common foe. For while ideological elements waver, the power factor is immutable.

Expediency will serve it in the future as it has done in the past. Upon the passions of East-West conflict in loyalties and ideals, in class and culture, dispassionate judgment by the Kremlin seems remote. Yet we do not now have to grapple with any weird, incendiary compound of national skulduggery and native frenzy such as the German mountebank dished out to his admirers, at home and abroad, as Nazism's solemn *mystique*. In their propaganda of misrepresentation and in their coercive machinery of mass conformity, totalitarian governments, Right and Left, are as alike as two peas in a pod. But there is nothing in Communist exhortation or practice which apes the peculiarly Germanic cult, trumpeted forth with the frantic acclaim of the Nazi hordes, of war for war's sake. Among the ideological antagonisms and diverse interests which have driven East and West apart, this is not one. And that, too, may be why some pacific standstill has, in theory at least, been more feasible with Russia than it ever was with Hitler, and even though it has for its precarious sanction only a stabilizing deadlock in competitive power.

What would be the repercussions of such a pause within the Soviet Union itself? World crisis may be a waiting game; but despite the triumph in China of satellite arms, and provided there is no economic recession which gets out of hand or recovery measures are not whittled down, time can still be made to work for us. Though Communists have dusted off and polished up the imperial tradition of Peter the Great, they have, unlike him, closed the windows of Muscovy to the West; the magnetic spectacle of a less rigorous and more beneficent way of life would be too unsettling. In Soviet assemblies, popular deliberations are for official propaganda and assenting nods; in the democracies of the West, the people retain power by delegating it. For among modes of government, only the representative system can be inherently self-perpetuating; only within it does incumbency depend not on individual men of power but on the institutional power of men. Between rival pretenders to the throne, dictators may or may not pass the scepter down without bloodshed.

But while their domestic tenure might be maintained by foreign crisis, a domestic crisis always lies dormant within it. And because crisis within a crisis—the latent inner crisis of every dictatorial regime—involves the ambition of rulers more than the interests of the ruled, the lancing of this fester by unrest at home can be postponed but never finally avoided.

With any widespread *détente* abroad, and with the Kremlin thus not as able to exploit internally foreign perils which it had aroused against itself, the domestic problem may come to a head. Though their encroachments diminish or change direction, a totalitarian government must, for its home effect, want to go on shaking the fist at an allegedly hostile world. Incongruities of that sort are, as we know, not confined to dictatorships. But if they become too much even for a people as stringently kept under and as viciously misinformed as the Russian, Soviet potentates might save their own skins, not through a war in which they also must go down, but simply by ceasing to live dangerously. Rather than as prospective organizers of an unattainable victory, they could appear before their own people as the benevolent artificers of a decreased tension—one which, in the age of air-atomic warfare, is for them, too, the most precious of boons. And by plowing back into production for peace a military potential which sharpens the contest of power, the country may prosper and the regime profit. But the more the latter lightens the shackles, the less its own life expectancy. For revolution—or the revolution against revolution—is as apt to occur when national fortunes begin to improve, when the oppressed can bestir themselves for freedom, as when the nadir of misery or tyranny is touched. But that is a river to cross when it is reached, and it is far, as yet, from sight. Meanwhile, recalling Hitler's fate and not wishing to repeat it in a Kremlin air-raid shelter, even commissars might wish to die in bed—a less unlikely demise as they also escape the vengeance of the wronged, the mob's fury, and the hangman's noose, because, to men of peace, much had been forgiven.

In ancient days the Mediterranean world was divided when it could not all be conquered. And it will be recollected how, before their sun had set, Pope Alexander VI drew a line of demarcation between the imperial spheres of Spain and Portugal. So now, in our own postwar era, a settlement between the United States and Russia, which could be more than an armed truce, has always been available —available, that is, on Russia's terms. Yet for that, too, there is a recent precedent. Hitler, in the autumn of 1937, offered to Neville Chamberlain's emissary, Lord Halifax, a partition of the world between Britain and Germany—the former to have a free hand outside Europe, the latter to have a free hand inside Europe. But while the European balance could not thus formally be forfeited—and while most of the overseas world was not Britain's property to barter away as she wished—the Chamberlain government, to the misguided applause of millions, proceeded during the next year, and without compensation, to bestow on Germany in substance what they had ostensibly withheld in form. For all warnings had gone unheeded. And when Europe's balance of power, with which Britain's own independence is wrapped up, was not protected by policy at an early stage, it had, under the most adverse of circumstances, to be defended later on by arms.

And now, as the Truman Doctrine, the European Recovery Program, and the North Atlantic Pact proclaim, Europe may be abandoned by treaty to Russian domination as little as to German. Against the ascendancy of Russia, the rest of Europe can by itself no longer maintain any balance of its own; western Europe is, however, a vital factor in that larger world balance by which Russia is restrained and peace is preserved. To renounce the whole of Europe to Russian predominance would be for the United States to nullify associations twice hallowed by common victory; to desert allies whose national freedom is not their heritage alone but that of civilization; to strengthen the East while paring down the preponderance of the West and tying its hands where it can least afford to have them tied. It would, in short, lessen the diplomacy of peace by power and increase the chance that only through war may the world contest be decided.

This problem can be examined from yet another angle. Two

worlds exist. Their frontier, however, runs at least through the middle of Europe, and not around it. By refusing, moreover, to recognize the validity of the exclusive spheres which obtain in practice, the United States keeps open the door to a wider peace settlement between all victors irrespective of size, geographical situation, or ideological bent. And in the same manner the Western Powers, by pursuing a policy of that sort, reserve the right, exiguous at the moment though it be, to exert their influence everywhere in Europe.

Nor is it certain that a two-world pact, if one were signed, would be observed. Overtly, through Communist parties abroad, and covertly through the Comintern's successor, the Cominform, the Russians could violate any self-denying ordinance designed to prevent either signatory from intervening ideologically or politically in the other's sphere—or in areas which may be formally neutralized. Not that the West should delude itself about the vigor of the democracy that might yet blossom in countries which have never been renowned for it; but neither should we hamper ourselves from supporting any nationalist discontent that may quicken under Moscow's lengthened shadow. For ideological penetration, as an aspect of the power struggle, is a game at which more than one can play.

The overriding prize of the world contest is, nevertheless, civilization itself. For as we determine who is to possess most power over or within it and how that power will be used, we compete among tangibles for what ultimately are intangibles. In a civilization of power, ours is an endeavor to preserve the power of civilization. Nations and empires may wax or wane; economic systems and concepts of society might evolve and alter. But civilization itself, because it both comprehends and transcends these, would, if laid desolate, be hardest of all to resurrect. The brain reels and the heart is sick over what can now be done by the weapons and machines of the twentieth century to human life in the aggregate, to the physical structure of the modern world, and to the intellectual heritage of men which it mirrors and by which it is shaped. Yet since from their ravages neither victors nor vanquished would be spared, the chronic pressure and counterpressure of power politics may not be a prelude to war but a substitute for it. Political *ersatz*, it will, moreover, until there is a moral equivalent for war, be better at least than the original article.

Culture follows the flag. Accompanying the outward push of Russia's power and Soviet doctrine is a way of life which, under czar and commissar alike, has a style and stamp of its own. The common stock would be poorer without the music, the literature, the dance, and the drama of Russia; without that which was devout and creative, much that is picturesque and even barbaric, in the Slavonic genius. Yet, though an important tributary, it must not become the main stream of Western thought and expression, one which might overflow its banks and sweep all before it. Through Byzantine and Judaeo-Christian influences, Russia drank but little at the Hebraic, Greek, and Roman springs of Western civilization; in her semi-Asiatic seclusion she missed the spiritual tumult of the Renaissance, the Reformation, the Enlightenment, the English, the American, the French revolutions—their effect on the mind of the West, on its customs, its laws, its modes of government, and its principles of freedom; on the progress of science and discovery, of scholarship and critical inquiry; on technical inventiveness and on its material application all the world over. And now as Russia again expands, a threat similar to that of domination by Germany looms up once more. Being tyrannies, neither might countenance the personal liberty and individual opinion which are the lifeblood of civilized society. But while the dynamics of German and Nazi imperialism were always such that you either had to crush it or be crushed by it, Russian power has been deflected and can delimit itself; and while the Germans had acquired more of a Western veneer than the Russians, the declared objectives of the Soviet Union seem closer to our own. Yet they are not our own. For since ends and means interact, they are finally inseparable; and when the latter are bad, they taint the former.

Let us not deceive ourselves. The imperfections of Western society cry out to high heaven; the discrepancy between what we could do but do not is only matched by what we do and should not. Our own transgressions are such that in ourselves we may deserve to put small faith; in the legacy of civilization handed down to us we must, on its own merits and by comparison with others, take pride. Its newest trustees, we have a duty to discharge to the past and, even more, to the present and future of mankind. In the contest of power before it, the West must vindicate the exercise of its power, not through a desire to impose it on others, but out of an awareness of what the world would be like if a worse brand of power were to prevail.

4

THE CONSOLIDATION OF THE WEST

America's Leading Role

IT IS THE PARADOX OF AMERICAN POWER ON THE contemporary scene that if the United States had been less passive in the 1920's and 1930's, she could afford to be less active in the 1950's. The shift from a European to a world balance she neither sought nor desired; no Great Power ever accepted a bigger, if lonelier, role more belatedly or with more reluctance. Her first considerable modern venture into world politics began during the era of the Spanish-American War, over half a century ago. And it was statesmen as prescient as John Hay and Theodore Roosevelt who then perceived what this entailed. For John Hay, with an eye on China, realized, like Jefferson and Madison before him, how others such as Britain had furnished the United States, as she forged her national unity and as she acquired colonial possessions, with a saving equilibrium in Europe and a protective barrier on the oceans. And while Theodore Roosevelt's reflections were of a somewhat different character, he did attempt, as did no previous American statesman, to mediate in a major European crisis so that in the Pacific region neither Russia nor Japan might, after their conflict, become strong enough to menace his own country.

The thinking of these men, the founders of American foreign policy in the twentieth century, had to be done within the traditional framework of power politics. Woodrow Wilson, however, amid the flux of general peacemaking, could combine this with the more collective approach of a later epoch. But neither Hughes, Stimson, nor the early Hull who followed, could go as far; it took the perils and the waste of another war for the American people to set their feet on the same path again. The Washington administration under Harry Truman inherits broad internationalist policies bequeathed them by Woodrow Wilson and Franklin Roosevelt. But the opposition party in supporting bipartisan measures can also invoke an authentic interventionist outlook whose necessity, despite the purblind interlude of the twenties and thirties, some of their own Republican predecessors were the first in this century to appreciate.*

What, however, could not be foreseen, either by them or by anyone else, is what actually came to pass. With the defense of the Western world resting in the main on American shoulders, the historic position was reversed in which the day-to-day overseas security of the United States reposed on the power of others—a power which in final emergencies she might later reinforce or even supplant but never continuously share or underpin. Between the wars, statesmanship almost everywhere was at a discount. Nor will it do to lay all the blame for the misdeeds and miscalculations of public figures in Europe during those years at the door of American isolationism—a circumstance which nevertheless estranged France after 1919 from her chief allies and encouraged the resurgence of militant Germanism. With the English-speaking peoples on both sides of the Atlantic sedulously cutting their own throats throughout the period, there is no assurance that the power of the United States would have been exerted in Europe as wisely as in eastern Asia. Yet if it could not only have been used but used with intelligence, with energy, and in consonance with moral, if unratified, commitments to France, Germany might never have gone berserk again and Japan would thus have been easier to subdue; and if war was not averted in Europe or the Far East, it might at least have been waged without so dire a sequel.

For a fundamental premise of the Founding Fathers, one which

---

* An account of the diplomacy of John Hay and Theodore Roosevelt is contained in Gelber, *The Rise of Anglo-American Friendship*.

John Quincy Adams and James Monroe took for granted, and one on which, from the turn of the century until the 1940's, isolationists and interventionists could alike proceed, has ceased to be valid. This was the predication of a world order in which the United States dwelt, yet which, except at critical intervals, others might largely maintain. For while Americans disputed over whether or not they should remain aloof, they all, implicitly if not explicitly, relied on its existence. But the pillars of that world order, shaken badly after 1914–1918, could, after 1939–1945, no longer stand by themselves. And that is why the self-rejected stone of American power has had, as it were, to become not only the keystone of the arch but its base and girders. No movable buttress to be shifted from the building after a storm, the United States is now fixed in her place as the mainstay of the West against a rival structure of power.

Here, then, is the underlying significance of the transition from a continental to a world balance. Until the 1940's the contest of power, though world-wide in its ramifications, was at heart European; today, while Europe still weighs heavily within it, the world equilibrium is one whose two outstretched poles are actually or virtually non-European. And nothing since the Declaration of Independence has done more than this to transform the stature of the United States. For the result is a change in her world function: the fact that when there are no others left in the West to do so, she is compelled to discharge unremittingly a world function commensurate at last with her world power. And so, lest there be no freedom anywhere, she has jettisoned one of her own most cherished freedoms, the freedom to act or not to act, now or later, as she pleases. For act she must—at once, incessantly, and always.

This applies to the settlement of the second World War and to every aspect of postwar international relations. It would apply no less in the event of a third world war being unleashed. In the past the United States could abstain for a while, as she did from 1914 to 1917 and from 1939 to 1941. Henceforth, and whoever fires the first shot, she would be embroiled as a principal belligerent from the outset. Until 1939 it was the full participation of imperial Britain which made world wars out of local or continental ones; to that role also the United States has now fallen heir. Operational lines in such a future catastrophe are impossible to forecast. But diplomatically, the front lines which once went through London, Paris, and Berlin, go now through Moscow and Washington. Formerly, the United States was caught up indirectly, and it was her prospective associates who were directly involved. From now on, even though they still unhappily first bear the brunt, it is they who will be brought in indirectly and through the initiative which, as leader of the West, the United States herself must henceforth exercise.

Yet preeminent though the United States may be in world affairs, it is an oversimplification to depict the East as having been held in check solely by her power or to suppose that this was summed up in the manufacture by her of the atomic bomb. The atomic bomb, with or without guided missiles and bacteriological warfare, was the gravest of known deterrents—until the even more infernal hydrogen bomb had been broached. What prevails is the over-all preponderance of the West. And that consists of many elements—political, strategic, economic, intellectual and moral.

Yet what in the light of the postwar contest of power would have happened to the liberties of Europe if the Air Force of the United States had not cast its atomic bombs on Hiroshima and Nagasaki? For Japan in war then, for Russia in peace afterward, there had to be some conclusive proof of their devastating potency. Through her spies, Russia had been apprised of our secret work on atomic energy and thus helped along in her own rival undertaking. But if we had not divulged the existence of the project, and if we had not known that the Soviet Union knew about it, the atmosphere in the West today would be one not of vigilance but of a fool's paradise whose dangers cannot be exaggerated. The West, anxious to return to a peace footing, crippled its own postwar power diplomacy by an overrapid disbandment of its military forces. But the Russian Government, which creates more than it responds to the popular will, confronted by the internal stringencies of a desolated land and the external temptations of the European power vacuum, did not demobilize its service personnel as much or as quickly. Under such conditions the atomic bomb must have been a stabilizing factor of inestimable significance—until, at any rate, the West could again steady itself. Other factors would soon also make themselves felt: strategic air bombing may never have been an exclusive capacity of the West's; but in the early postwar period, while our amorphous power was recrystallizing, even a temporary atomic advantage enabled less impermanent deterrents to reassemble along with it.

Historically, it is of profound importance that a redistribution of world power which leaves the Soviet Union on top in Europe and Asia coincides with the progress of invention elsewhere. Together with the Soviet Union's own industrial plant and some of Europe's, the East's untapped resources might be as enormous as the West's and its armed man power far in excess. It does not only rank below western Europe and North America in steel and heavy industry— those prime indices of military power—but does not compare with them in scientific, administrative, and engineering proficiency. As Russia, with the subjugated plants of eastern Europe, with her own heavy industry and her Five-Year plans, is to India and China, with their larger populations but lesser productive capacity, so is the West to her and her satellites. In any race between the nature of Eastern man power and the power over Nature of Western man, the latter, provided it does not yield its technological superiority, can stay ahead.

Outside Europe, the West enjoys access to most of the overseas non-Soviet world—even to portions of Asia and Africa in relative proximity to the Russian land mass. For the Soviet Union can supplement its vast fighter arm with an atomic air arm of long-distance strategic bombers; its German-designed submarines may expect to wreak havoc with Western shipping and troop movements; expendable Russian infantry and heavier mechanized armor, with bigger and more numerous artillery, may push across the face of Eurasia and into the continent of Africa—to the North Atlantic at one extremity, to the Indian Ocean and the South Pacific at another. Yet dispersion of its forces, and therefore diffusion of its force, must exhaust even the seemingly inexhaustible Muscovite giant. With the West pounding from the air at selected vital centers, the bad transportation over tremendous distances, the managerial inefficiency and material insufficiencies, the oppressive conditions under which the Russian people and their subject nationalities live are all bound to register. In surface sea power, in heavy bombers which might fly above or beyond the range of intercepting fighter planes, the East cannot match the West. If an early lightning offensive in the air-atomic age would be a reckless gamble because of the instantaneous punishment which the West might be able to inflict on Russia from surrounding bases, a long-drawn-out war may be precluded by the stupendous resourcefulness of the West, its unique faculty for outlasting an enemy once the battle is joined.

And it is behind this screen of world power that in western Europe the West has been putting together again the tattered remnants of its continental power. In the annals of the Soviet Union, Marshal Stalin's fame will be that not so much of a revolutionary as of a post-revolutionary figure. It is, oddly enough, in American history that he could go down as, so to speak, a revolutionary *pur sang*. For under his aegis the Politburo's course of postwar Russian expansion has at last stirred the United States into countering with no temporary alliance in an extraordinary emergency but with an entangling one—the North Atlantic Security Pact—of long duration, and one of the sort against which Washington and the Founding Fathers themselves adjured her. A miracle which neither three emperors, William II, Francis Joseph, and Hirohito, nor a European dictator, such as Adolf Hitler, could accomplish in two world wars has been wrought by the master of the Kremlin with comparative ease and by striking a series of oblique blows in peacetime. Pearl Harbor was the turning point. But while isolation ended there, the postwar commitments of the United States have, like the Charter of the United Nations, been general in character; confined to the Western Hemisphere through the inter-American system, as expressed in the Rio de Janeiro and Bogotá agreements; or restricted to North American defense arrangements with her Canadian and Mexican neighbors.

The first step toward a specific military alliance in Europe was taken when Secretary of State Byrnes proposed his four-Power treaty to keep Germany disarmed. When this offer was ignored by Russia, something more was required than the visit to Turkey of an American battleship or the promulgation of the Truman Doctrine. A second step was therefore taken to preserve that *status quo* in the West which victory over the Axis embodied.

An armed attack against one or more of the signatories in Europe or North America being considered an attack against them all, the principle of the Atlantic Pact is that of mutual aid and reciprocal assistance. For purposes of rearmament the corollary arms and companion economic recovery policies of the United States have been to help those who help themselves. With the industrial capacity and strategic position which western Europe can thereby contribute, the prospect is also one of each helping the other; on the Scandinavian-West Europe-Mediterranean sector of the world front, the defense of North America itself is thus bolstered. Locally this process of military convalescence is also rendered feasible by the American air-atomic force stationed in the British Isles and protected by the Fighter Command of the Royal Air Force; safeguarding the armed truce on the ground is the thin brown line drawn across the middle of Germany by the American, French, and British armies of occupation. For without their salutary vigil the Soviet Union might have reacted with violence when the North Atlantic compact affronted her continental hegemony. To brush aside that frail human rampart or trample it down would be to release a maximum of counterpressure in all elements and from every direction overseas. Fragile in itself, it is strong in what, when defied, it symbolizes and may prefigure.

To what extent can continental members of the North Atlantic Alliance, rearmed and reequipped, be counted on to do more than absorb the first shock of war or fight a delaying action? France remains the key. But with the French still torn internally and Indo-China a drain on her power in Europe, with the Low Countries indecisive, with Norway and Denmark exposed directly to invasion, they will each have done much if they can defend their own territories until other of their Atlantic Allies either from there, on land and in the air, or elsewhere, by sea and in the air, mount global reprisals. For the advent of mechanized and technological warfare leaves them with but little room in which to maneuver against a mass onslaught. Russia, on the other hand, has the whole terrain of eastern Europe and her own wide tracts across which, if pushed back, she could once more retreat. Nor is it possible to predict the full strength that the island of Britain, as she staggers under the ill effects of her two recent wars, can exert. The scope of Anglo-American air and sea power in sustaining the United Kingdom, and in carrying the attack from there and from western Europe to the enemy, will be affected by the amount of Russian air and sea power which would accompany the westward sweep of Russian land power. Since the Middle Ages, a foe holding the Low Countries and the Channel ports pointed a dagger at the heart of Britain; true again in 1914 and 1940, it still is true. But the last war showed how such an adversary might also devastate her ancient towns and modern factories by waging an air offensive from more distant bases in Germany and Scandinavia.

On the other hand, in an assault on western Europe an aggressor from the east must operate at the end of outstretched supply lines and far from tactical air bases of his own such as the Atlantic Allies can have in western Europe. This time, moreover, the Rhine barrier would not be behind, but ahead of, an invader—one whose cumbrous power, unless western Germany had been aligned with it, must be mobilized, not in adjoining territory, but in the most distant part of the Continent. The object there of the Atlantic partners is to equip a moderate number of mobile combat divisions which would be an élite in training, armor, and guns, with adequate reserves and supported closely by fighters, fighter bombers, and dive bombers—Britain providing the larger jet-fighter needs of the continental armies. Alone, this smaller force could not stem a Slavonic or Teuto-Slavonic flood indefinitely. But it could man the dikes long enough for three things to happen. First of all it would allow Anglo-American tactical air power to gain command of the air over the onrushing forces of the East. Second, it might permit additional land troops from other Atlantic Allies to be speeded to the side of the defending divisions. And third, the encircling pressure of strategic air bombardment of the Soviet heartland must slacken the fury and lift the weight of a Russian onslaught in western Europe until the hour when the West itself can take the offensive.

Without the rearmament and military restoration of western Europe, there could be no Atlantic Pact. For if the East-West contest were played out solely in terms of the strategic air power of the United States, as reinforced by American sea power, the nations of western Europe, even though liberated subsequently, would have to resign themselves to yet another occupation from the east. Without assistance against invasion, there would be no resistance to it; by surrendering beforehand to the conqueror or his domestic Communist collaborationists, the western Europeans might obviate much personal sorrow and suffering. The total defense of the West, on land, at sea, and in the air, is what the Atlantic Pact implies. But unless western Europe is psychologically prepared by its military renovation to fight for its own liberties until others come fully to its rescue, the over-all power of the West itself will have been impaired. Nor would the war vessels of the Royal Navy be able to use the ports of Canada and the United States as a haven if western Europe failed to resist. Blackmail of the populace of the British Isles by terror from the air might compel even that historic armada to return to home waters and yield.

As a matter of fact, American strategic air power should not want to depend exclusively on non-European bases for its own operations. The war policy of the West would thus be one in which global and continental factors of defense are interrelated and coordinated. Western Europe can, moreover, probably be strengthened before Russia has manufactured atomic bombs in large quantities and before Germany's reawakening nationalism dons either a military or Russo-Germanic guise. For there is a clear moral obligation on Anglo-American legislators and policy-makers, who have sponsored the Teutonic rebirth, to assist France and western Europe with compensatory defensive measures. If the revival of the German economy saves the American taxpayer from expenditure in one direction, some of the charge in the other for rearming apprehensive allies must be assigned to just that policy. But since the Atlantic Pact and American arms may give western Europe a sense of security, they are in themselves a further fillip to economic recovery and to that extent a premium on insurance which concurrently repays itself.

Is a North Atlantic Alliance too late in trying to do in the middle of the century what should have been done thirty years before? The ghost of Clemenceau, sardonic, impassioned, prophetic, might rise up and remind the American people that common interests are not new; that the bargain he made as a reward for major French concessions during the 1919 peacemaking was broken; that in addition to Article X of the Covenant of the League of Nations, on which the English-speaking world afterward poured scorn, the security of France was to be underwritten by the most exact of Anglo-American commitments; that his thrice-invaded country would be strong today, the Hitler nightmare and Russia's ensuing continental predominance avoided, if the Treaty of Guarantee he had signed with Woodrow Wilson and David Lloyd George had been ratified by the Senate.* Nor could he pass over in silence the spectacle which Britain was later to present, until, for her follies, one of the two prospective guarantors of 1919 has herself now also had, as it were, to be guaranteed.

Yet the Atlantic Pact is neither a guarantee of frontiers nor a precise commitment. As a statement of conjoined policy it is a watershed in history. With it the United States serves notice that she will not again wait for her ships on the high seas, her oceanic possessions, or even her home territory to be attacked; that none can subscribe once more to the belief of the Kaiser before 1917, and of Hitler before

---

* Article X committed signatories of the Covenant to preserve the territorial integrity and political independence of members of the League. To amend, remove, or neglect that Article was to emasculate collective security as the prewar generation understood it. The Charter of the United Nations, directed more flexibly to the maintenance of international peace and security, contains no political or territorial provision as rigid and therefore as far-reaching.

1941, that even if their course did embroil the United States they would by then be entrenched in their domination beyond dislodgment. By it the Congress and the administration together are set free from outworn tradition to act in the common interest as soon as they see fit. But they are not free from each other. With its insistence on national sovereignty, its refusal to be committed automatically, the treaty demonstrates how small is the impression made by advocates of an Atlantic federal union. What, above all, is imperative is that within Washington itself, as between Washington and allied capitals, there should be no pedantry of interpretation or jealousy of rights which might retard the immediacy of the pact's potential force in diplomacy, its actual force in war.

For though casuists split hairs, common military preparations do establish a moral commitment. In the July-August crisis of 1914 the British cabinet discovered that because of previous naval and military arrangements entered into with France under the Entente understanding, they were no longer free agents; that in addition to national interest there is also—as M. Cambon, during agonizing hours of doubt, recalled to Sir Edward Grey—national honor. And now, too, not even the most eminent of senators could eat their cake and have it. For on a crutch which might, in a moment of need, be pulled out from under them, the lamest of our European allies would not want to lean. They can either rely on the United States and Canada or they can come to terms in advance with a probable enemy. The Executive and Legislative branches of the American government have had to decide which alternative they desired. For their treaty must mean everything or it means nothing. There is no midway point.

The strategic unity and economic aid which accompany the Atlantic Alliance thus bespeak more than explicit, all-inclusive stipulations ever could. For legal technicalities enshrined in archaic processes of government are a minor element among the political realities to which the pact attests and conforms. Before the defense of the Constitution comes the defense of America; more important than the eighteenth century American division of powers is the twentieth century unity of the Atlantic Powers. Anglo-American friendship, the old Entente-

Alliance tie between the French and the British, the new Brussels Treaty, the historic brotherhood-in-arms of France and America, Canada's long sought trinity of herself with Britain and the United States—all these special groupings, with other selected relationships, can now combine, interpenetrate, or reassort themselves under the impact of events and within a prior and broader institutional framework. For the *Pax Britannica* which underwrote the progress of the West in the nineteenth century, and the *Pax Anglo-Americana* which could have done the same in the twentieth, have now been replaced by a *Pax Atlantica*.

Politically and in principle the pact is said, under the Charter of the United Nations, to alter little. Operationally and in time much is changed by it. And never was time, in this age of atomic-hydrogen bombs, guided missiles, supersonic air speed, and armor on wheels, more of the essence. But at my back, sang the poet, I always hear Time's wingèd chariot hurrying near. Seldom has the imagery of romance been more literally or unromantically fulfilled. For the machines of men have not only foreshortened time; their chariots are in fact wingèd ones. And it is here that some anti-Soviet critics of Atlantic power politics go awry.

For it is their argument that economic reconstruction and a more just social order are what will afford stability to western Europe, as indeed to many vulnerable corners of the earth. Generally, and in the long run, they are correct. Yet between power and plenty there should be no false antithesis. It is not Communist ideology alone against which, in restive non-Soviet lands, we must be on guard, but against such ideology as the subversive forerunner of direct or indirect Russian military aggression. And it is by these twin Soviet activities that the rhythm of economic or material recovery can be outpaced; before a nation's well-being is improved its political independence may be extinguished. Never were time and timing as much a function of power. And in that respect also the Atlantic Alliance is an effort by the West to steal a march on the East; to pool strength so that recuperative forces may have an unobstructed chance to do their work. For between social justice and the West's preponderance there is no dichotomy. Without the latter we cannot get the former. And to relinquish it will be to cast overboard much else besides.

Censure of Atlantic power politics on such grounds, though mistaken, is legitimate enough. It is harder to be patient with one set of liberals in the West who, despite Russia's abuse of the veto in the Security Council of the United Nations and the Soviet extirpation of all liberties within reach, disparage the West's system of defense as a gratuitous provocation of so peace-loving and so law-abiding a stay-at-home as the Soviet Union. Yet, quite apart from Communist party members and their fellow travelers, men of this mentality are no phenomenon without precedent. Before 1939 with many, until 1941 with others, their prototypes enabled the Nazis to make immense strides forward because it was contended that the Germans were only redressing just grievances; that it was not so much their munitions-makers as ours who instigated wars. The revisionist school among historians and writers on international affairs thus inculcated the sanctimonious delusion that, since one side in the European crisis was as bad as another, they should all be dismissed with a plague on both their houses. In the face of the most vicious illiberality which ever extended its organized sway, abstention was urged as the liberal choice for America. In an unfree world, what had been the home of the brave could, alone and by itself, still be the home of the free.

In the Senate and among distinguished publicists most spokesmen for this self-anointed poltroonery have recanted. In the universities, however, anxiety is now expressed over pro-Soviet teachings. But those scholastics whose prewar books and pedagogy did so much to confuse the public mind about the nature of world affairs, those eunuchs of the spirit, the intellectual precursors of America First, they have lost no credit by errors at once so profound and so prolonged in learned influence. Ensconced and promoted through professional seniority, the squatter's rights of corporate education, rather than proved merit or vindicated judgment, they and their coteries often still rule academic roosts.

Certainly it is not for men of that sort to indict the escapism of the Baldwins, the MacDonalds, the Flandins, the Daladiers, the

Neville Chamberlains. For the retreat of Europe—accelerated so needlessly by them into a rout—began when the United States herself repudiated the achievements of Woodrow Wilson. The world issues were as clear in 1935 and 1939 as they are now; American public sentiment was such that Franklin Roosevelt, despite his call for the quarantining of aggressors, signed in those years two Neutrality Acts which gave the Axis *carte blanche*. For while the Italian conquest of Ethiopia, the further Japanese attacks on China, the remilitarization of Germany, the reoccupation of the Rhineland, the rape of Austria and Czechoslovakia were milestones on the road to war, so was this American legislation. A green light to aggressors, it notified the Axis that at the outset, anyway, the United States would not pull her weight, that in defense of the West there would be no common world front. Through the Anglo-American deal of bases for destroyers in the summer of Dunkerque and by his antisubmarine order to shoot on sight, Roosevelt himself did his utmost later to circumvent his own fateful signatures. More specifically and more concretely than the United Nations Charter, the Atlantic Pact is, nevertheless, on a semiglobal scale, an American pilgrimage to Canossa. For the common front of 1917–1918 which, after 1941, had so painfully to be rebuilt, is again in being. In its absence war was not averted. By its existence peace may be preserved.

From Versailles to Pearl Harbor the free world pleaded with the United States to pursue a more positive course abroad. Yet now that she has emerged from isolation and taken the lead, the pro-Soviet complaint is not the disuse of American power but its misuse. That she will do too little rather than too much is still a danger which may protract and intensify the crises of peace. Cheeseparing in the Congress over recovery and arms programs, the calm assumption that American legislators enjoy more than their foreign partners a diplomatically and strategically wasteful privilege of delay, are a perennial source of disquietude to the allies of the United States. For the latter, having cast in their lot with the West and having incurred thereby the wrath of the East, must be sure that they can count unremittingly on the fullest backing from across the Atlantic Ocean. American action that is dilatory, lukewarm, or reluctant thus exacerbates the very crises which action that is prompt, wholehearted, and complete could assuage. Yet the fact that in any potential scuttling of responsibility, in any national self-constriction of American foreign policy, the diehards are reactionaries of the Right and not statesmen of the moderate Right, the Center, or the Left, shows how false is the charge that the United States, however it may grope and stumble, has embarked on a selfish career of old-fashioned imperial greed. Isolationism makes strange bedfellows, but only the perverse rectitude of a Senator Taft could gratify both the Wilhelmstrasse before the war and the Kremlin after it.

And now it probably is true that in setting up her countervailing structure of world power the United States has poked her nose into the domestic affairs of allies and wards, that in paying a socializing piper she has been tempted to call a capitalistic tune. But unlike what happens within the vicinity of Russia, if they are irked in their independence they are also fortified; and though kid gloves are not *de rigeur* in Washington, neither is a fist of mail. Even if American leadership had ripened, not in the East-West's fierce, noonday schismatic glare but in the mellowing sun of a more settled epoch, there would be *gaffes* and missteps. When, therefore, fault is found with details or even, as over Germany, with major aspects of policy, it is proper to observe that the sum total of American efforts is to preserve by common action in peace that freedom in the West which, without her at last, would have been lost in war. It is late, but not too late, for the United States to do that now for which the civilized world has prayed during most of this century. And only the interests of Moscow are served by the self-defeating perfectionism which, after lamenting her isolationism yesterday, upbraids her interventionism today and treats as wrong whatever she does.

Among some non-Communist intellectuals in Britain and France, such querulousness would have occurred under any circumstances in which their countries, celebrated for centuries as the chief world centers, have to play second fiddle. But it is not only the pride they must swallow and the humility they must affect which the United

States should understand. Americans themselves are often baffled by a system of government which bids the administration negotiate but not commit and branches of the Congress to commit but not negotiate—with no assurance, even when the party complexion of the Legislative majority and of the White House is the same, that consent to ratify will be forthcoming. For the division of powers which is designed to preserve American freedom at home could again result in such a division of power abroad as would hinder larger freedoms.

From John Hay to Woodrow Wilson, as the United States began to assume her modern world rank, it was a question whether, under the Senate's two-thirds vote on treaties—under a minority veto, that is, of one-third plus one vote—she could give a durable, unbroken lead. But if the passage of the United Nations Charter was to pick up the threads where Wilson left them, the Atlantic Pact is akin to Hay's concept of Western unity—a grouping that would also have been formed against an expanding Russian despotism and into which the militaristic Germans could not fit. For cooperation between the Legislature and the Executive did improve during the Axis war years; prior consultation with influential senators and the bipartisan approach enables the congressional system, like its parliamentary counterparts, to register more democratically the straight unfettered will of a simple Legislative majority. These, however, are working arrangements of a transient character which may or may not become a permanent convention of the Constitution. Yet unless they do, the diplomacy of the Russo-American epoch may have to ask itself not only whether we can do business with Russia but also whether the United States herself can do business.

What will be the world pattern of the next five decades? Unless the political intervention of the United States can match her productive strength, there is not likely to be an American Century; from suburbia to superbia the road is military as well as cultural. The threat to the twentieth century has been that of being Teutonic in the first half, Slavonic in the second, and free in neither. And if the American people are served less effectively than for their own and for the world's sake they ought to be, the problem is not merely one of out-moded eighteenth century procedures in a twentieth century milieu. It is also one of competence in those who get their hands on the machinery of government. For in diplomacy content and execution are inseparable; how and when a thing is done counts almost as much as what is done. Under General Marshall as Secretary of State there was less of the soldierly discipline than had been anticipated as his particular forte in the administration's conduct of affairs. Over the Middle East he and Mr. Lovett were not averse to sabotage of the President's line; nor was James Forrestal, whose tragedy of misjudg-ment—and of thus being misjudged—would end with the judgment of tragedy. Over Germany an imperious Clay-Draper proconsulate went unreproved when it contravened directives to deconcentrate those gargantuan industrial cartels which in peace as in war had sucked dry the lifeblood of Europe; when it condoned the early return to influence in a reconstructed Germany of the most unre-constructed Pan-Germanic elements. Inside and outside the Adenauer government these might, moreover, still have been curbed if the initial complaisance of the first civilian High Commissioner could not be traced to prior Stimson-McCloy policies in Washington itself.

Nor in an emotionally charged atmosphere can American democ-racy work rationally if all remonstrance against such forcible-feeble zigzags is attributed to Communist inspiration. Some of it might be. But it may be less sinister and more patriotic to recollect who have been the enemies of the West in two recent wars and might yet be again. At any rate the frenetic rebuilding of a unified Germany owes much to Anglo-American functionaries, outwardly so hard-boiled and inwardly so naïve, whose misdirected Right-wing materialism is as downright as that of the Marxians—Social Democratic and Soviet—themselves.

So as to shatter no idols, Mr. Truman, after his election, eased out gently, with honey rather than vinegar, dissidents of eminence and thus sealed off diplomatic as well as martial undercurrents of top mutiny. For diplomacy should be the vocation of men with appro-priate training and not the avocation of those who confound administrative energy with knowledge and wisdom. The subordination of military to civil authority, as General Eisenhower once reiterated in a classic document, is one of democracy's cornerstones; nor does foreign policy operate unaccountably in a void apart from those who handle or mishandle it. In its determination, as in its discharge, it must be centered, fully and precisely, somewhere. Unless the power that goes with responsibility is itself responsible, the anarchy of Washington can only deepen the world's anarchy.

The leadership of the West, a legacy to the United States from Britain and France, is the supreme art of politics. After being accustomed for generations to compensate with pronouncements of principle for the exercise of power, the American people have suddenly had to discover that neither one will do without the other. And the spirit in which they are fused is important. For leadership has its duties to perform on low levels as on high. The political democracy of the British at home has often been contrasted with the manner in which the white man's burden is shouldered by them in their colonies. A different sort of inconsistency is now chalked up against English-speaking officials serving in the German occupation. One reason, it is said, why Germans show no remorse for the cold-blooded slaughter of millions of fellow mortals in their murder factories is because Americans, as well as British, on the spot, intimate to the local populace something less than the utmost reprehension at this characteristic feature of that Nazism in which so many Germans reveled for so long. Yet democracy can be no stronger than the moral fiber of its exponents and no safer than the intelligence they reveal. Furthermore, as Germanic bestiality goes unrebuked, German power thrives; and as German power thrives, the preponderance of the West is itself imperiled.

Blots on the American escutcheon mar but do not obscure what is otherwise a fresh postwar luster. Totalitarian dictatorships have been a setback for humanity of which Europeans, with their great past, can scarcely boast; it is not for them to sneer at any relatively innocuous countinghouse mentality displayed by Americans engaged in a common endeavor to promote the economic recovery of another continent. The import policies of the United States should be liberalized before a minatory attitude toward Europe's fiscal controls and splintered economy is warranted; as Europe becomes politically more secure, private American and European investment must continue to drive the pumps which the European Recovery Program has primed. Washington on other issues may falter and fumble. In western Europe the era of Soviet-American ascendancy might be decried as one of parvenus. But on that brand of statesmanship, neither before nor since the war, have the United States and Russia cornered the market.

Britain's plight is proof of this. Despite a more coherent system of government than the American and despite national interests that are more vulnerable, she has long lacked the requisite world leadership. Except for the resplendent war period of Winston Churchill, with some prior assistance from Anthony Eden, there has for over two decades hardly been a prime minister or a foreign secretary who, whether on the Right or the Left, could measure up to the high traditions of his office. For obsolete machinery functions if qualified men work it. Better machinery will be of no avail if sound conceptions of policy are not arrived at in time and diligently pursued.

Nevertheless, the parliamentary as distinguished from the American presidential system in countries such as Britain, France, and Canada does furnish for cabinet appointment men, even of ordinary caliber, who have at least already won their spurs in public affairs. There, as elsewhere, on the Left as on the Right, these things are also decided by caprice, by connections, by a host of "available" factors other than ability or suitability. But a government whose life depends on majority votes in Parliament itself, and which confers rank on ministers who sit in the Chamber, tends to consist of a politically more seasoned type than that which the White House may recruit direct from business or the Armed Services. The separated powers of the American Constitution thus produce not only a perpetual crisis in matters of policy, but also in the selection of personnel. In both Houses of Congress today there are some who have had to work their own way up the ladder, who learned in a free society to appraise public responsibility as the public appraised them, and whose political sense would be more statesmanlike and more continuously useful than that of the "practical" outside colleagues with whom Presidents often surround themselves. For while cabinet or presidential specialists may enter at the top, they have no place in the Legislative machine where afterward they might still remain; they have no place where, once a specific job is finished, they can make their experience felt until, as in a parliamentary system, other similar posts are again open. And yet from the point of view of democracy that may not be an unmitigated loss. For men who have not risen by their own efforts within a political chain of command —with its electoral immediacies and parliamentary intercourse— might incline, when too enamored of office, to miscalculate or overstep its real, if indefinable, limits.

Yet whatever the defects of democratic leadership, no totalitarian substitute, whether on the Right or the Left, has done or can do as well. Normally our representative systems pick out and exalt that mediocrity in which the mass of men sees itself and with which it therefore feels at home; by thus registering its own will, however, it also confirms its own freedom. And that is why the mediocrity which dictatorships impose is worse than that which democracies prefer; individuality is leveled down in both, but only in democracy is there a simultaneous counterprocess by which it is fostered. As the contrast between the Roosevelt-Churchill era and its postwar sequel indicates, the hour does not inevitably produce the man; or rather, while democracy may produce the best men, her nod is bestowed on them too seldom. Nevertheless they are there, and in emergencies it does beckon even to them. With more of them we should do better. With fewer we would do worse.

As a struggle for power the Russian blockade of non-Soviet Berlin exemplified the rule of war through weakness, peace through strength. That particular episode of the East-West schism terminated, momentarily at any rate, when the Anglo-American airlift and the Allied counterblockade, causing economic distress in the Soviet zone of Germany and elsewhere in eastern Europe, had made its prolongation futile. But during 1948–1949 the Russians would not have hesitated—or would not hesitate again—to shoot Allied aircraft out of German skies if the visible evidence of Western resolve were not a mere token of more that was as yet invisible; if the answer to small-scale action there would not be full-scale action everywhere. The power of Anglo-American logistics lay in the logic of their total power. For the gauge of power is whether, in any final test, either side must relent. When there is an array of strength which renders war not only unprofitable to both but more unprofitable to the war-like than to the unwarlike, peace by power results. Yet if the issue had been forced in July, 1948, before the West's own new structure of power was ready, before the Atlantic Pact could try to crown the recovery process and give Western Europe further confidence, the outcome might have been a military and inflammatory rather than a diplomatic and sedative one. To use the convoy with which General Clay first wanted to smash through the Russian zone would have been not an affirmation of power, like the airlift itself, but to be rash and premature in its employment. The preliminaries of the West German Republic might have been the occasion rather than the cause of conflict. Yet not having recuperated from waging war to destroy German power, the peoples of the West were almost plunged into war to restore it.

When Berliners in the Allied zones spurned Soviet blandishments during the blockade, and when a considerable number of Germans there and in eastern Germany voted against national unification under Russian auspices, the Allied governments had better cards with which to play. But we should be hoodwinking ourselves if we imagined that in renouncing the East the Germans will unalterably embrace the West. They can hate Russians, as they always have, without loving us. Whatever else they may or may not understand, they do respect the lesson of power. Sheltered by a successful demonstration of Anglo-American power—a peacetime spectacle denied other peoples subjected both to Nazi and Soviet tyrannies—Germans might hope to extricate themselves from a Russian yoke. At this stage cooperation with the West is more likely than cooperation with the

East to offer prosperity and real independence. Freedom for Germany rather than for Germans is what, after all, they have invariably sought—although the one without the other has signified freedom's eclipse, national and individual, for everybody else. Yet once their independence is achieved under the shield of the West, once they have regathered strength to deal with Russia on more equal terms, they can throw us over again as they have thrown us over before.

As we let the Teutonic genie out of the bottle, it begins to exercise added weight in East-West contention. The pressure for unity, stimulated by us at Frankfort and Bonn, may, in swerving from one direction to the other, sweep its own foreign promoters off their feet. On VE Day, as the horrors of what Germans and what Germany can do were still being divulged or unearthed, few would have guessed that among Washington legislators, American recovery administrators, and occupation officials from the United States the deleterious London atmosphere of the 1930's would be so swiftly duplicated. For the European balance of power was permitted by helmsmen of the same stamp, and contrary to the most vital interests of Britain and civilized society, to swing against their own heedless country and against the entire West. So now, and despite warning voices, the rebuilding of a powerful German state will shove into the talons of the Soviet Union the one means it needs to erase the very preponderance we are intent upon maintaining against it.

On this question, however, the Atlantic Pact, with its reciprocal obligations, accords France that special hearing the lack of which was Hitler's chief asset. For, together with the other Brussels Treaty Powers, unless France stands firm, the Atlantic Alliance can have no land-based application in western Europe; and she will not stand firm if her morale is sapped again as it was after the German blood bath of 1914–1918. The European Recovery Program, Anglo-American arms assistance, and the general provisions of the North Atlantic Pact contribute to the stability at home and security abroad which are essential to her strength. Yet as Communist disaffection within is combatted, the threat of a new Vichy may arise from the strategic pattern we ourselves adopt, not only across the Rhine, but across the

Channel and below the Pyrenees. For since, as the West's first line of defense, France has not been sure of herself, some in Washington have wondered whether it would not be better for the Allies to concentrate in Europe on an air defense centered on the island of Britain and behind the mountain barrier of Spain. Not that the British could rejoice at a strategy whose premise is the deployment of Russian land power along their historic moat and on the Atlantic coast of France. But France, bogged down already in Indo-China, will scarcely have the heart to resist an invader if her Allies are preparing in advance to abandon her to another remote, speculative, war-disfigured liberation. Nor will Belgium, the Netherlands, or Italy. Instead, by letting her Pétainists of the Left at once take over, France herself might try to salvage something from the wreckage. With France—and thus Germany—falling to the Kremlin, and with Britain isolated, the domination of Europe, which the Atlantic Alliance is to deny her, would have become Russia's anyway.

Such being the strategic prospects, ideological qualms over whether or not to deal with Franco or with a Francoist regime can be exaggerated. The democracies of western Europe, having writhed under the Nazi lash, oppose any contact which would further Fascist Spain, the last prewar protégé of the Rome-Berlin Axis, and its wartime accomplice against all of us. Historically, their position is well founded; ideologically their own skirts are not quite clear. For none could be morally so fastidious as to refrain from a wartime alignment with Russia, which also had collaborated with Hitler; or, because the Soviet bloc is totalitarian, to declare it ineligible for membership in the United Nations. Portugal, Britain's most ancient ally and now one of the Atlantic Powers, is Fascist; not every member of the United Nations in Latin America or every signatory of the pacts of Rio de Janeiro or Bogotá is a paragon of basic democracy. Nor were all the elements in Germany, with which governments in the West have been associating themselves, exactly martyrs under Hitler to the cause of freedom; within the United Nations we have trafficked with feudal Arab dictatorships which were not only pro-Axis but which, unabashed, have since waged war against the decisions of that world body. The democracies of the West, having themselves thus let expediency outweigh principle, can scarcely insist upon ideological yardsticks. But if the debate on Spain were to induce a more thorough soul-searching among some self-styled ideological purists, it might help cleanse the air.

Raised in the context of power, the topic of Spain should be disposed of by the same criteria. Can Madrid offer the West a reasonable military advantage without levying too exorbitant a toll—diplomatic or economic? The answer may not be entirely in the negative. With Spain's benighted, ill trained soldiery and bad transport facilities little could be done; for rearmament and reequipment, our Atlantic Allies must, on all our overseas resources, enjoy a prior claim. Franco may not be persuaded to lower his price of full admission to the company of the West. Yet conditions in Spain are such that he might be well advised to settle for less. And if we could purchase rights to footholds in Spain, the transaction should be of a commercial rather than ideological nature. But additional European outposts in that corner of the critical Mediterranean area must be to implement and not replace the territorial defense of France herself.

For bases in Spain should not cost us more psychologically than they are worth strategically. And this consideration, while ostensibly ideological, is in fact one of power. For no rapprochement with Spain will be judicious if it leaves France or our other West European allies skeptical of American intentions; if they conclude that, before they have been assisted to resist invasion, the United States is preparing to retire to a second line of defense on the outer rim of the Continent. There may be those who doubt the capacity of western Europe to survive a frontal assault by Russia; who deplore efforts and materials devoted to remilitarizing western Europe as a diversion from the main task of rebuilding the gigantic military machine, especially in the air, of the United States herself. But the alternative is to write off western Europe completely; to take from Anglo-American occupation forces in Germany their strategic hinterland; to remove a major stumbling block in the way of any Russian drive westward before its impact is felt.

For among peoples who are not separated by the broad oceans from the continent of Europe but are joined to it by land, narrow seas, or a common air, there lingers near the surface a wistful longing for a policy of neutrality, the fear of being ground between the upper and nether millstones of Russia and America, the illusion that the world contest instead of also being theirs is one between the two mightiest of adversaries alone. War-weariness and the politics of despair could, after two world wars, thus invite a third; and in supporting the old West economically, diplomatically, and strategically, the new West repels a defeatism fatal to Europe, damaging to North America, detrimental to the preponderance of the entire West, old and new. A historic venture in power politics, the North Atlantic Security Pact is also one of those exercises in morale, in the imponderables of politics, which can direct power and justify it.

Over Germany the misgivings of our European allies have, with reason, been acute. Designed to protect the West from the expansion of Russia, the Atlantic Treaty can operate no less against the resurgent Germans. Yet an Anglo-American policy which restores German war potential while offering military security to France and western Europe may be doing two things which are not only at odds but which, in canceling each other out, could obliterate the civilization they are supposed to preserve. France, it is argued, should welcome a big German obstacle in the Russian path. But will it be an obstacle or a steam roller which smoothes the way? For while such unreliability as France may manifest springs from internal divisions which can be healed or surmounted, the more Germany is united, the less reliable she becomes. And that is why she can neither be trusted with arms nor admitted into the Atlantic Alliance, why we may have been putting dynamite under the walls of Europe as we shore them up.

A Russo-German combine is the one event which more than any other could bring the perpetual East-West crisis of our era to a head. Britain, as in 1940–1944, would do her utmost to protect her sovereign independence. But the West European portion of any world balance will have collapsed irretrievably. All that could be looked

for in Eurasia would be an equipoise such as its two European masters subsequently establish by agreement, by rivalry, or by conflict
between themselves. For between world contestants the Teuto-
Slavonic East may overrate its chances of victory. Peace by power
has prevented war. But the preponderance of the West is its buttress,
and if that vanishes, so may the peace.

From similar projects adumbrated in the past, the Atlantic Alliance
differs in many respects. One innovation, broadening overseas leadership in the preponderant West, is the new world stature of Canada
as a junior guarantor at the side of her senior North American partner. Another is that, unlike the 1919 Treaty of Guarantee, which
died aborning on Capitol Hill, or the 1946 Byrnes proposal, it is
reciprocal rather than unilateral in its incidence; not a particular insurance against the military revival of Germany but a general commitment against all aggression in the Atlantic area. With its larger
number of specific beneficiaries in Europe, the inclusion of Britain
among them is, moreover, a woeful comedown from the proud
days of Canning and Monroe; an epochmaking reversal from that
great century when, whatever her relations with the North American Republic—or the nascent polity of Canada—she herself might
either offer to be or could, with her pervasive sea power, tacitly remain the real guarantor of the security of the Americas. It is thus, too,
a far cry from that Anglo-American world alliance—with or without
imperial Germany—to which John Hay and Joseph Chamberlain
aspired and which, if implemented as between strategic equals, might
have saved twentieth century mankind from the ravages of two wars
and so banished the shadows of a third.

In Europe and Asia the elements of crisis are similar but not
identical. Between the paramountcy in China and in eastern Europe
of the Soviet Union there are parallels; the problem of colonialism
and the recession of empire in southeastern Asia contrasts with a renewal of power among the free countries of western Europe. A
slower tempo in reunifying and rebuilding Germany having been
desirable, is the same caution called for in our treatment of Japan?
There could be no doubt of the answer if the goal of current policy

were simply to protect ourselves against the vengeance of both Germans and Japanese; if our task were only to remember that, as faithful democrats, the emperor-worshiping Japanese as much as the goose-stepping Germans have yet to show that they are anything more than Johnny-come-latelys. But in the Orient, as in the Occident, the East-West power struggle takes on the color of its environment. As Japan is revived industrially and given more of a free rein politically, the Philippines, which she subjugated, may be estranged and their advocacy of a Pacific regional pact would also have that in mind; within the Commonwealth and within the Far Eastern Commission, the influence of Australia and New Zealand has, in this connection, been unsympathetic to the United States. For the attitude of these Pacific countries—Canada's security being the same here as that of the United States herself—toward Japan is roughly comparable to the attitude of France, Belgium, the Netherlands and Luxembourg toward Germany. But Australia, uneasy over Sino-Soviet progress, now takes the view that in industry and trade Japan should become self-supporting, that much of what Asia needs she must provide.

For while Germany demolished Europe's order of power and Japan destroyed East Asia's, the one may no longer be potentially as dangerous as the other. The essentials of Germany's former strength will soon be back within her own grasp; they may be utilized, when the hour strikes, as she sees fit. Strategically, the islands of Japan have mostly been deprived of theirs.

For while Japan's air and sea power were tools of conquest up and down the Pacific, the Japanese Army was, and always had been, the chief instrument of her aggressions. Throughout this century the more Japan anchored herself on the continent of East Asia, the more unruly she became. Imprisoned in her islands again, stripped of the territorial foundations of Far Eastern power—such as the unified Federal German Republic retains in Europe—Japan today is divested of the main weapon of her military prowess. Until the war of 1904–1905 the Russians were dominant in Manchuria and Korea; with the diplomatic assistance of the Anglo-Japanese Alliance, in the first revision of which President Theodore Roosevelt then secretly participated, Japan overthrew the forces of the czar and accelerated on the East Asiatic mainland her own swift, upward climb to mastery.* From the eve of 1914 to the aftermath of 1945, no earlier doctrine of the Open Door or of Chinese sovereignty and territorial integrity, none of the principles of the Paris peacemaking or the Covenant of the League of Nations, none of the Pacific treaties signed in Washington, no toothless Kellogg-Briand pact to outlaw war by moral incantation, and still less any melancholy rhetoric of mere verbal protest from Messrs. Stimson and Hull were enough to stop Tokyo. Nor was the lesson lost on Rome or Berlin. And when America, so remote from danger, would not act, Europe—and Geneva—could not.

The year 1939 may have signalized the defeat in Europe of the cause for which in 1917 the United States went to war. But in China her discomfiture has been virtually self-administered. For there, too, where she had long taken more of a lead than in Europe, the American people fancied that peace could somehow be self-enforcing. They caviled at the truth which John Hay, Theodore Roosevelt, and Woodrow Wilson, each in his own vein, perceived: that in even the most high-minded formulation of policy the language of power lends power to its language.

Might there, then, be verisimilitude in any self-portrait which Americans paint as that of a nation of unmuscular sentimentalists hardened by Pearl Harbor into one of sentimental toughs? Not as much as they would like to make themselves believe. For in external relations they, too, have long been tough. But toughness of mind does not connote breadth of mind and the United States has been more diffident over her extracontinental security than she has been in foreign affairs nearer home. The Spanish-American War, America's substantial contribution to *fin de siècle* imperialism, was followed by its Panama epilogue. But what has been forgotten is that, before this last occurred, Congress threatened the crass, unilateral abrogation of treaty rights which envisaged an equal partnership

* The important contribution of Theodore Roosevelt to the making of the second Anglo-Japanese Alliance is described in Gelber, *The Rise of Anglo-American Friendship,* pp. 217–250.

between Britain and the United States in any isthmian seaway. The administration, in coaxing London to abandon those rights, thus had the backing of the Legislature for a display of power politics beside which the chancelleries of Europe, reputedly past masters of the art, must have paled with envy. The hemisphere assertion of American power, as Canada also learned at the time, was the precondition for any Anglo-American unity of power.* For what distinguishes recent from former foreign policies of the United States is not so much a shift from complete isolation to full participation as a move from the self-engrossed regional exercise of power to the affirmation of power on a wider, grander, more cooperative scale.

Meanwhile, the current rebuff to the United States in China is not merely political or commercial. It is also strategic. Much will happen and more must change before the military power of China could be organized by the East against the West. But the victory of the Chinese Communists stretches and loosens the defensive ring Russia has compelled us to draw around her. And it preserves Soviet Asia from the land-based counterpressure which the air power of the West, if allied to a Nationalist China, might have exerted from nearer continental points in the Far East when Russia's own expansionist pressure was excessive elsewhere.

At any rate the pendulum which once swung away from Russia and toward Japan has now swung back. Outer and Inner Mongolia are satellites of Russia's and so is Sinkiang; through the Yalta agreements Manchuria and half of Korea—the latter having passed into Japanese hands with the consent of Theodore Roosevelt—are hers in all but name. For the treaty of mutual aid signed on February 14, 1950 between the Soviet Union and Communist China cannot expunge the effect of Muscovite severities meted out to Chiang Kai-shek less than five years before. The apparent control of the Manchurian railway, of Port Arthur and Dairen, returns once more to the country from which they had so often been wrenched.

* For isthmian power politics in Anglo-American relations, with their crucial bearing on the Alaskan boundary dispute with Canada, Gelber, *The Rise of Anglo-American Friendship*, pp. 37–58, 86–108.

Russia will still possess there the reality of power. But toward south-eastern Asia and in conjunction with Moscow, Peking may essay to make up at the expense of others that which it cannot fully retrieve nearer home.

For China could not be to eastern Asia what the Brussels Treaty Powers may yet be to western Europe; and that, in the Far Eastern phase of the postwar crisis, has been one of our chief difficulties. If we do enough to reinforce our European Allies, we strengthen them and ourselves; in China, short of an all-out military campaign with which even the Chinese people might not have cooperated, it was impossible to bank on the same result. In the Occident, moreover, our major foe—Germany—lay next to Russia's sphere; in the Orient it was our friend—pre-Communist China—whom the latter borders and has enveloped. The frontiers of the free world could not, then, be demarcated as clearly in Asia as in Europe; nor could they, if fortified in time, be as surely defended. In China the likelihood of doing that had long been dim. During the Axis war, with which the Sino-Japanese struggle merged, we urged her to fight on against what had become a common enemy. But some of us demurred when, in an excess of zeal, her Western spokesmen depicted her as spiritually more advanced and as politically mature as ourselves. At San Francisco she was granted one of the five permanent, veto-power seats on the Security Council—a world rank for which, whether as Kuomintang or Communist, China has never had the capacity and which, therefore, could not be in the best interests of the United Nations itself.

The wrongs China has suffered have been twofold—those inflicted by others and those of which she or her own sons, despite the culpability of foreigners, cannot be exonerated. It would be unfair to carp because her decrepit civilization, at once so rich culturally and so backward socially, could not suddenly adjust itself to the unbidden techniques of the contemporary world; in all the contests of modern power her uninterrupted ordeal might have been duplicated elsewhere if others had been as vulnerable geographically, as solitary politically, and as chaotic administratively. Blame for the evils wrought in China since the close of the nineteenth century must be widely shared—the unequal treaties and foreign concessions, the annexation of ports, the carving up into spheres of interest, the rivalries which confused, and the invasions which laid waste. Britain and France may have taken the first steps in this respect. Yet over half a century after the Opium War it was a British government, when others were entrenching themselves more deeply in China, which proposed to President McKinley political guarantees of China's sea-coast territory. And it was a commitment of that type which alone might have saved her from the worst consequences of her own past debility —one which would have prevented the trials not only of her Nationalist epoch but the entire heartrending tragedy of China since the turn of the century.

The fact is that sins of omission, like those of the United States, were a standing invitation for sins of commission—breasts being beaten where sabers should have rattled, and sabers thus rattling where all should have been still. In shaking ex-President Hoover and Senator Taft from a hands-off policy, the Formosan uproar of 1950 did what was not done by Japan's invasion of Manchuria, by Hitler's conquest of Europe, or by our Atlantic defense structure against Russia; on world affairs their batting average was as low as ever. Not that every American policy-maker from McKinley to Knox and from Hughes to Hull has known how he was hamstrung in the Far East or by what; even Hoover's Secretary of State, Henry L. Stimson, was prone to denounce Sir John Simon rather than his own country's self-emasculating isolationism for errors that were not one-sided. Yet the makeshifts in which Washington had to indulge sprang from that, as from no other comparable factor—until having been damaged so rudely in 1931 at Mukden, they blew up at Pearl Harbor. For in Asia or Europe no order of security is automatic. And that exercise of power which might have kept it intact may no longer suffice for any mere reversion to its initial, unbroken state.

Nature, too, furnished China with little alleviation. To the flood of disaster was added the disaster of floods. And then came the heavy blows of the postwar period. At Teheran, when victory was still only a blueprint, Mr. Churchill, commonly regarded as the most adamantine of imperialists, expressed willingness to discard one of the rooted policies of the British Empire and, to solidify the Great Power concert, approved of Russia's historic claim for access to warm-water ports. Mr. Roosevelt, with the presumed assent of Generalissimo Chiang Kai-shek, suggested that the Manchurian port of Dairen be internationalized so that Russia, replaced there in 1905 by the Japanese, might regain it as an outlet.* But the post-Yalta violations, the undisguised imperialist rapacity of the Sino-Soviet Pact, Russia's plunder of Manchuria's industry—a province to whose full retrocession China was entitled—brought morale low and set the stage for the progress of the Chinese Communists. And then Russia, after despoiling Manchuria in 1945, engaged herself in 1950 to restore much of the loot, both property and sovereignty, to the regime of Mao Tse-tung. But the economics of puppetry being what they are, the change is more likely to be one of form than of substance.

The English-speaking peoples may be appalled at what after Yalta had to be done to humor Russia, not only in eastern Europe, but also, so as to ensure her further cooperation prior to the fall of Germany and the atom-bombing of Hiroshima and Nagasaki, at the expense of China. Yet on the Russo-German war front there reigned an ominous lull. Yalta might have been the price paid to Generalissimo Stalin by Messrs. Roosevelt and Churchill to forestall another Nazi-Soviet Pact—one which would unloose on the British Isles and on our troops in western Europe the full fury of the latest German weapons and the final impact of the undivided Teutonic mass. At any rate, in no other manner, among the terrible unknowns of the time, could global victory or postwar peace be envisaged.

Nor have the Chinese themselves been guiltless. The setbacks provided by Nature, foreign intrigue, and Japanese aggression were not alone in dissolving the pattern of reform which Sun Yat-sen inspired. They were helped along by feuding war lords; by the early re-

* Sherwood, *Roosevelt and Hopkins*, p. 792, also pp. 866–867.

fusal of Chiang Kai-shek himself to patch up his quarrel with the
Chinese Communists so that there might be a joint defense of Manchuria against the Japanese; by the failure of governing circles to
ameliorate some of China's primitive economy and set an example
of sacrifice in the midst of a ruinous inflation; by their extinction of
moderate counsels behind a mummery of representative government;
by an antiforeign sentiment devoid of the spirit of patriotism or
national unity; by the conviction of the Kuomintang that, because
of the East-West schism, the United States would have to back them
whatever the circumstances of civil war or domestic tyranny. Elsewhere than in China, in eastern and Central Europe, most Communist
regimes have been minority groups which took control when Russian bayonets stood near by. In China the armies of Mao Tse-tung,
General Chu Teh, Liu Shao-chi and Chou En-lai unfurled their ban-
ners over areas far beyond any into which Russia or Russians had
ever penetrated. Nor were the Chinese Communists, unlike others of
the Soviet sphere in Europe, a minority group in their own districts
or provinces, but, as in Yugoslavia, a dictatorial movement with
popular support promising the wretched multitudes a lighter yoke
than that of the Kuomintang.

And that is why the United States, which has rushed to the aid of
menaced regimes elsewhere, could do nothing to rescue Chiang Kai-
shek's. For when his troops deserted to the Communists with American arms and supplies, what they lacked was not matériel but gen-
eralship, loyalty, a cause for which to fight; and these no alien government, however sympathetic, could provide. To have helped the
Kuomintang repulse China's enemies was one thing; it was quite
another to bolster the losing side in a huge civil war; to assist in
fastening a crumbling and discredited regime on the overladen
shoulders of tens of millions of disaffected Chinese themselves. For
that would be to drain away the strength of the West, when it is
needed elsewhere, without steeling China against the East. Indicative
of her new realism, above all, is the fact that as the United States
dropped the anti-Communist Kuomintang, she offered limited military assistance to the anti-Russian Communists of Yugoslavia. For

when, as between contending regimes, ideological issues are so be-fogged, power alone might be of some use.

Her new masters, however, if they are more Chinese than Com-munist, may eventually try to rid their country of all foreign trammels. The Russians have neither oil nor machines to spare for the industrialization of China; only in the West can these be ob-tained. And it is questionable whether they or their Russian mentors possess administrative gifts which could develop a land so enormous, so inchoate, so encrusted with ancient folkways, in the full mold of their ideological tenets, or as a decisive acquisition of power by the East against the West. A Communized East Asia cannot therefore be to the Kremlin what a reunified and reindustrialized Germany may soon have become. Immobilized as a partner of the West, China might yet even be a deadweight to the East.

This, however, is conjectural. So, too, is Chinese revulsion should Peking and Shanghai also be exposed, as allies or co-belligerents of Moscow, to the Pacific air strategy of the West. But it is clear that the economic loss to the West, if southeastern Asia falls into the Sino-Soviet lap, will be as great as, if not greater than, the political repercussions. Yet even its strategic raw materials must still be sold on world markets—though not through existing preferential channels. The Russians can neither purchase nor consume all of them, and, unless others do, the general discontent of satellite peoples on the perimeter of the Soviet realm will smolder and mount.

We cannot wash our hands of East Asia. But it is a knack of states-manship to put first things first. The affairs of China and Europe have been interacting for more than five decades. When the West, reinsured through its global defensive system, devotes itself neverthe-less to one main theater, while the East concerns itself with several, it manifests that tactic of concentration which, in power politics as in warfare, is the secret of success. And besides, since Russian land power, like German land power before it, operates on interior lines, its own mobility will slacken as, among the peripheral races of the Orient, it stretches out too far. For while some of the nationalisms of Asia might genuflect toward Moscow as they strive to evict the empires of the West, the intrusion of Russia should ultimately prove no more congenial. Wielding rough brooms of borrowed doctrine—the East's ideology of social revolution, the West's ideology of political revolution—the revolutionary nationalism of the Orient may seek at long last to sweep out all interlopers wherever they originate.

Is Japan, close to Manchuria and better situated than American bases on the Pacific, a vantage point from which the Occident could still exert power in East Asia? The severance of Japan from the Asiatic continent heralds her divorce from the springboard of conquest. It also means that she is cut off from a principal source of food for the teeming populace of her overcrowded islands and from raw materials which her reviving industries would have to use. Since Japanese can no longer emigrate, the practice of birth control might assuage national misery in Japan, as in China and India, by reducing the size of the population. But a less dependent economy in Japan requires trade outlets, the lowering of tariff bars, and capital investment. The American taxpayer, with other urgent fiscal burdens at home and abroad, might to some degree thus be relieved of a most onerous one across the Pacific. And if Japan were also to have her own armed forces again, they could police the country against a Communist uprising or invasion from the mainland. Yet each one of these steps, each stage of relief thus procured by the United States Treasury and the National Defense Establishment, could not only be of financial and military value to the West; they might constitute an entering wedge for that restoration of Japan's war potential against which all Pacific Powers are pledged. For the problem is one of getting Japan to stand on her own feet without stamping on everybody else's. And to that problem no watertight solution is discernible.

Hazardous though the rehabilitation of Japan may be, it is not as hazardous as the rehabilitation of Germany. The United States does, after all, occupy Japan almost alone and has, despite the Far Eastern Commission, had her own way there; the occupation of Germanic territories is shared not only with Britain and France but, across an artificial boundary, with Russia herself. As long as the United States, with her other Pacific bases and associations, maintains her supremacy on the sea and in the air of that region, she might safeguard her own foothold in Japan and prevent any vengeful regime in those islands from again pursuing a hostile course. A revived Germany could be more recalcitrant. As her strength grows, it attenuates the control which the West can assert within her and decreases correspondingly the potential effectiveness of that which, through the Atlantic Alliance, is being assembled outside her frontiers. But if Japan were ever again to resume her traditional militarism on the Asiatic mainland, she would crash there against the new continental power—the Kremlin's and now also that of Peking—by which she has been so fully displaced. With an industrially rehabilitated and politically unified Germany the situation is dissimilar. For a renewal of German expansion would be at the expense not of Russia but of western Europe and the entire West, not as Moscow's rival but as its ally.

A chastened, unwarlike Japan has, however, more interests in common with near neighbors than distant conquerors, and these they may be glad to foster. Strategically, Russia would want her to remove herself from the camp of the West. But as long as American occupation forces steer the Japanese ship of state and American subsidies keep it afloat, it cannot have a Communist government or one on the Left that might join up politically with Communist China and Communist Russia. Yet in Asia, as in Europe, power is no respecter of ideologies. Even a Right-wing Japan, emulating for nonmilitary purposes the Germans and the Soviet Union, might strike a bargain with the Chinese People's Republic. Yet with Russia herself Japan can look forward to no special ties. The deficit economy of Japan may function either on an American dole or under its own steam when it has access to the resources and markets of the Asiatic mainland. Yet there is no exact analogy between a reviving Germany and a reviving Japan precisely because a new Rapallo is more probable between Russia and the former than between Russia and the latter.

After the Russo-Japanese War of 1904–1905 when Japan was the victor and Russia the vanquished, St. Petersburg and Tokyo did make such an agreement. Then, however, it was Russian power that was contracting and Japanese power that, on the East Asiatic mainland, was expanding. Theodore Roosevelt had labored for a speedy settlement lest Japan wax too mighty; his design for the security of the United States on the Pacific and in East Asia was predicated on the future counteraction, at no cost to his own country, between the two erstwhile belligerents. North American writers are still fond of referring to what they call "balance-of-power politics," as though somewhere, somehow, there was another less wicked, strictly non-European brand. In fact the United States had always exploited a favorable distribution of world power. But under Theodore Roosevelt—and after John Hay's pioneering efforts—she attempted for the first time, and during interconnected European and Far Eastern crises, to reshape one sector of it in her own national interest; to frame actively rather than accept passively its regional modification. Theodore Roosevelt then suffered the pangs of a hemisphere power politician without real world power; Woodrow Wilson would have power for war but not for peace. Yet it was the same American isolationism by which both statesmen were frustrated. Prior to 1914 czarist Russia and Imperial Japan were each allied to a member of the Franco-British Entente; against the Central Powers of the Triple Alliance a quadruple grouping was formed—with an understanding in Asia as in Europe between the partners. The device by which others would preserve for the United States an equilibrium in the Pacific area was thus stultified almost at once, and Japanese inroads in China increased.* Many years later, when the United States had to intervene in the Far East with full force, it was a reinvigorated Russia and not the United States herself which profited most.

And this fact, as much as American occupation policy, must decide the fate of Japan. For hitherto the understandings which governed a chronically violent Russo-Japanese relationship were conditioned by the advance of the Japanese on the East Asiatic mainland and the

---

* The interaction of major European and Far Eastern crises, its effect on the pre-1914 policies of the Great Powers, are outlined in Gelber, *The Rise of Anglo-American Friendship*, pp. 167–275.

retreat of the Russians. Now, however, Japan is again bottled up in her own islands across the sea; Russia, in Asia as in Europe, is less vulnerable territorially than ever before; and while she herself might have filched rich Chinese provinces, most of China is being re-integrated under her patronage. A century's checkered interposition by the Powers of the West in the affairs of that hapless country has thus not only shriveled up and melted away; even if the Kremlin so wished, the hour has gone for a predatory Russo-Japanese agreement as in the past or on the traditional Russo-German pattern. Chinese nationalism, Kuomintang yesterday, Communist today, is a triumphant major factor in the Far East. To ignore it, as Germans and Russians have always ignored the rights of others who dwell between them, would be to push China back into those Western arms from which she has just been wrested.

Only in southeastern Asia are there third parties which might be the spoils of a joint program of Russo-Japanese exploitation. Yet to seize upon them, Japan would again have to become a mainland Power, again first have to overcome China herself. Without seriously entertaining a dual project of that sort, but as a Damoclean sword with which to dispel any inordinately Titoesque aberrations, Russia might dangle the prospect of one over the head of her Chinese satellite. Otherwise, while Soviet expansion is stymied in the Occident without the direct collaboration of a renovated foe, it has no such need of one in the Orient. If its own chosen instruments prove balky, so may Japanese militarists. And while in Europe a new Rapallo would be to the interest of both its signatories, in Asia it would only be to the interest of Japan. As internal foreign control over western Germany relaxes, her continental power, if allied to Russia's, will be beyond regulation. But whether the American occupation of insular Japan wears on or declines, Russia and China, no less than the United States, may externally now also regulate her reviving power.

Within those strategic limits, the outlook for an agreement would nevertheless be not unpropitious. Between southeastern Asia and Japan, as well as between China and Japan, the exchange of raw materials for manufactured goods can be arranged; with Japanese expert help the industrial productivity of the Far East, and thus its abysmal standard of living, might slowly be raised. The basic industrial supplies of Japan are located on the Sino-Soviet mainland; over her the United States still has the whiphand; unlike continental Germany, the Island Kingdom, walking a tightrope between East and West, can be wholly independent of neither. Nor would Communist China want to be too dependent on Japan as the workshop of Asia—not even if their doctrinal coloration, since power outweighs ideology, were to be of the same crimson hue. Never again, it may feel, should the small, lean tail be able to wag the big, fat dog; to dicker also with the capitalist states of North America or the semicapitalist states of western Europe may yet be for the Chinese Communists a simple matter of national prudence. In Europe, despite ideological dissensions, East-West trade proves necessary. Among the conformities of Asia it might be so no less.

Meanwhile Britain cannot recover by relinquishing markets and certainly she would be loath to make way for Japan, an old competitor from whose aggressions in southeastern Asia British interests suffered irreparably. But there will still be room for outside commerce if the whole area does not fall under a Communist heel. And here, as with the European Recovery or Greek-Turkish programs, power economics may again subserve power politics. If there is time, as the East presses down, the West might provide southeastern Asia with aid and markets without its having to mortgage the boon, so freshly won, of national liberty. For to be entirely trussed up in another closed Japanese economy or to be half-suffocated within a Sino-Soviet one may be as repugnant to Asian nationalism as was the imperialism of the West. But to be associated with the West economically while dissociated colonially might be to fulfill its own concept of freedom. And what the West forfeits in empire it may reacquire in good will—if not in power, then in the imponderables of power—while the East gains neither.

By itself, however, the leverage is small which we can exert on the spot to abate Russia's domination of the Far East. But the West has reserves of power to tap at other corners of the earth; and with these, in a showdown, the gravest damage could be done. For the more Russia's Eurasian land mass spreads politically, the more unwieldy it becomes. Puppet regimes in eastern Asia or eastern and Central Europe may decentralize her system administratively and socially; if their interests are overridden by those of the metropolis they might hinder as well as strengthen. At all events, unless subject peoples enjoy economic well-being and do not seem to have bartered one bondage for another, their reliability as servants of the Soviet must vary in inverse ratio to the proximity of Russia's own military power. And besides, the more the tide turns against the expansion of Russia in Europe, the more unencumbered the Occidental friends of Oriental freedom will be.

Not that a Pacific counterpart to the Atlantic Alliance has ever been practicable. Cultural homogeneity, such as exists between the chief members of the Atlantic community, may be lacking between the Orient and the Occident or within the Orient itself. Yet China, during the war and early postwar years, was admitted to the councils of the West; under the British raj the military and strategic contribution to the British Empire of united India was a solid one. Nor is the unfeasibility of a transpacific mutual assistance treaty due merely to the fact that none of the remaining Asiatic dependencies will honor the signature in their name of any sovereignty other than their own. The situation is plain. Neutral as between East and West, India herself is in none too robust a condition. There are no other free governments on the Asian mainland, as there are in western Europe, strong enough or stable enough to be a bastion of a common transoceanic defense. A politico-economic agreement of a looser, less specific character is what any general pact in the Pacific area must be. And since Asia is so much more backward than Europe, her regional or intracontinental distribution of power cannot as clearly determine the world issue. For what tells in the end is the total pressure and counterpressure of global power. And here the West is still predominant.

Attached to it, moreover, are countries like those of Latin America which come closest to the world contest through the ideological conflict within rather than the political struggle without, but whose further economic development would be in the common interest. Yet unless internal reforms are undertaken, unless wealth and privilege do their share there as elsewhere in the West, assistance from the United States and the United Nations may be to pour water in a sieve. For over a century the sea and air supremacy of Anglo-American power has, as expressed through the Monroe Doctrine, accorded Latin America the same hemisphere security as that enjoyed by Canada and the United States. In our two world wars for world order, however, Latin Americans did much less than North Americans; civil strife, a perpetual cycle of *coups d'état,* and the bloodiest of neighborhood wars have instead been localized for them. And provided that the Mediterranean and North Atlantic coasts of Africa are held by the West in depth, Central and South America will, even in the age of long-distance and air-atomic combat, still be one of the regions most sheltered by geography against the havoc of world war. The primacy of the West at sea and in the air must, in fact, align with North America, or keep within its reach and out of Russia's, all territories, whether or not affiliated with it politically, beyond the immediate range of the air-land power of the Soviet Union.

The task of correlating world commitments with world strategy is one which is imposed on the United States by her world leadership. Twice before she has sought to organize the West: once for peace under Woodrow Wilson and once for war under Franklin Roosevelt. What must now be done is so to organize the West for war that there will be peace; or so that war, if it nevertheless does burst forth, may be waged under the best possible, or least adverse, conditions. In fixing the size of American ground defenses in Europe, the United States, as the seat of power, must estimate not only the capacity of her Allies, the locale and the media to which her own fighting personnel are suited; she has to determine the respective amounts of air power, sea power, and land power which might be required on the exterior lines of a world front, or of world fronts, from which she herself, and no longer Europe, may be our directing or operational center. So, too, key transatlantic Allies of the Brussels Treaty group rather than former enemies should be favored economically, if revenues are straitened and budgets must be unbalanced as power is counterbalanced. For the object of the United States, within bounds decreed by her mammoth resources, human, material, and financial, must be neither to put all her strategic eggs in one basket nor to divide up her eggs in so many baskets that others can purloin them.

After the struggle of 1914–1918 and the armaments race which preceded it, the pacifist democracies rejected the ancient counsel that if you wish for peace you must prepare for war. *Si vis pacem, para bellum.* Theirs, however, was the dissent not of skepticism but of self-delusion, not of defense but of suicide. Mulish in their disbelief that others might not care for peace as much as they, the English-speaking peoples indulged in apologetics for their adversaries as these, thus inspirited, prepared for war against them. Neither in mind nor arms were the British and French ready in 1939, nor the Americans in 1941; after Dunkerque, if Commonwealth countries had not gone on fighting alone for a year until Russia also was embroiled, the United States might have been caught even more off-guard and denied time afterward to pull herself together. What we have learned is evident. To prepare for war may not ensure peace but it can prevent defeat. And if inferiority in arms would tempt aggressors to strike, the renewed preparations of the West should stay their hands.

Not that Russia could deem her post-Hitler exertions to have been fruitless. War would be a disaster as incalculable for her as for us. Yet by conveying the threat of war she has taken its gains while, by maintaining peace, she eschews its losses. And as war itself is averted, the Politburo can thus claim credit for having aggrandized their country through a prolonged exercise of power politics on the most colossal scale; for having played for high stakes and won much. The highest stakes of all—the liberty and destiny of civilized society—will still be in the keeping of the West.

5

RECESSIONAL

Britain and the Britannic Realm

In PRESERVING TWENTIETH CENTURY FREEDOM, Anglo-American unity has, among many variables, been the one constant factor. Yet, passing through numerous vicissitudes, it, too, has been more steadfast than steady. And though it has staved off submission by the West and is the backbone of our preponderance, changes have been taking place within it which affect the changing world equilibrium as a whole. The decline of Britain may be offset by the rise of the United States and Canada's greater capacity. The impairment of Britain's status and her relegation to a somewhat more subordinate role in international affairs cannot easily be compensated, even within the common, elastic Anglo-American fold.

For she has not only been weakened economically by her heroic war efforts and the further loosening of ties among members of the Commonwealth. The insecurity of France and all of western Europe would render her more vulnerable than ever before, even if she were not put in the front line of battle by the threat of enemy air power from the neighboring Continent. The Atlantic Alliance, as far as its two North American signatories are concerned, defines in writing a pledge for which neither sealing wax nor pen and ink might have been required. But the task today may be more complicated than when Britain took the lead. Sea power furnished a wider oceanic stability which could eventually blend with land power to win victory in western Europe; the East-West contest compels us now to scan the skies in every direction. The sea-land-air power of North America will still be brought to bear, though in altered proportions, on western Europe. But it has other frontiers, near and far, above no less than beyond, with which it must reckon and to which it may be diverted. That was also true in the Pacific war and of Anglo-American campaigns mounted against the Axis on the outskirts of Europe. But the weight Britain pulled then she might not be able to pull in the future. At a time when North America may have more to do elsewhere than ever before and when home territories may be under attack, its chief ally across the Atlantic is herself less strong.

Britain, within three decades of her 1919 victory, tended to be less the molder and more the sport of events. Between wars her economic difficulties had been grievous. Yet the way in which her foreign policies made things worse rather than better for herself should be an object lesson to every responsible citizen in every free democracy. Appeasement may have been an attempt of some among her propertied classes, as among France's, to conciliate the Nazis at the expense of Communism. It was, however, much more than that. The term evokes an image of peers and plutocrats jerking strings from stately mansions and the industrial Midlands, from the inner sanctums of the City, the Bank of England, and the *Times*, while in Downing Street their oracles minced and scraped. But this is at once too complimentary to them and too simple. To be sustained, national policies of that sort had to have a national backing which cut across party lines. For years it was the Left which, out of solicitude for Germany, fathered the indiscriminate revision of the 1919 settlement; a process of "peaceful change"—in the quaint, euphemistic language of the period—that appeasers on the Right merely borrowed and intensified. Having themselves broken the Versailles Treaty by their naval agreement with Germany, the latter condoned, while joining others in vapid gestures of protest, Germany's treaty-breaking rearmament, conscription, Rhineland remilitarization; and of these Austria, Munich, Prague, and Danzig were but the consequence of all that had gone before. What the Right did during the middle thirties was to restrain France when she could still protect herself. But on the Left, too, party and press acquiesced in steps which demoralized the French and spelled their doom—steps which were therefore to the obvious undoing of Britain herself. On both sides of the Atlantic, illustrious fellow-travellers of German ultranationalism had laid so much stress on the faults of the last peace that they had stupefied the West into letting peace go by default.

Prior to Versailles Britain had been one of the classic exponents of the balance of power, and her diminished stature is, in the end, due to her own subsequent misconception of that policy. After Napoleon I the Crimean and Prussian wars did not disturb the general peace; if the unification of Germany had not upset the balance of power, the twentieth century might, in this respect, have done as well as the nineteenth. Meanwhile British sea power, which, as the real force behind the Monroe Doctrine, had been shielding the post-Napoleonic growth of new countries overseas, localized the American Civil War, the Spanish-American War and the Russo-Japanese War. Yet when William II made his bid for hegemony, the German challenge to Britain was not only maritime and imperial but continental. It remained for her post-Versailles generation to flatter themselves with the monumental tomfoolery that they, quite apart from any League of Nations theory of collective security, had unearthed a secret of statesmanship, fresh, creative, infallible: that your enemies should be built up and your natural allies let down until, at the eleventh hour, other still more distant friends and Commonwealth partners must rush to pluck you like a brand from the burning.

For even after the advent of Hitler the British seemed to imagine that they could neglect or overlook the distribution of power on the European continent and yet manage somehow to retain their world power. They could, of course, do nothing of the sort. And their illusion was all the greater because their greatness had been no illusion.

Germany's second brief domination of Europe was, like her first, overthrown. But her anti-Russian, pro-Russian, anti-Russian alternations had terminated by bringing Russian expansionism into the center of Europe, while it left the western half of the Continent and the United Kingdom too enfeebled to restore alone that balance of power which had been the mainstay of their liberties and their independence. Aid has been forthcoming since Europe, the modern fount of Western civilization, is still the most decisive sector of the East-West contest. Geography in a dire extremity might permit the United States and Canada, as it never would permit Britain, to by-pass Europe. North America in the postwar period, and through the North Atlantic Pact, will do what the British, with catastrophic results, did not do early enough for themselves and their continental neighbors before 1939. Hitherto, in the final crises of the two German wars, Britain could fall back on the English-speaking peoples overseas to buttress the domestic pivot of her oceanic system. Now, however, the system of the free is an American one—the naval and air power of the United States having even become the principal sanction of scattered empires accessible by sea or beyond the reach of Russian land power. On home territory, when Britain and the nations of western Europe defend themselves, they also defend what they own elsewhere. Yet for the first time they are supporting, and being supported by, a world system of which they are a vital part but which is not primarily theirs.

Still possessor of the greatest of colonial empires, still foremost in a voluntary Commonwealth of independent nations, still the main associate in international affairs of the United States, Britain's future power, her value as ally or partner, is bound up with the manner in which, with the help of her friends, she extricates herself from a predicament so largely of her own making. In addition to history and sentiment, two other interconnected elements figured among the ties which have prolonged the attachment between herself and the sovereign countries of the Commonwealth. The first was the pride derived from being affiliated with a kingdom, preeminent at home in the rule of law and parliamentary government, whose ideas of freedom were carried by many of its sons to new lands. The second was the confidence bred by a guardian sea power which interposed itself between remote communities and any who might have designs upon them.

Yet in their own dependencies the British, despite the lesson of the American Revolution, often did most to obstruct the adoption of their own principles; the liberties of Commonwealth countries had first to be extracted by some, such as Canada, before being conceded to others. And it was this cycle, combining with more progressive trends in Britain's own public life, which furnished that odd, bewildering sequence of illiberal behavior in conquered regions, the maintenance of a liberal world order which her imperial and maritime power facilitated, the liberalization of many of her conquests. For whatever the attractions and repulsions which attended their birth or growth, Commonwealth countries patterned themselves politically on the model of Britain, transmuted much of her old empire into a fraternal body of sovereign equals, and looked to London as the chief exemplar of a common tradition.

Will they do so indefinitely? It has been the "inarticulate major premise" of the Commonwealth that Britain herself remain unsurpassed as an active Great Power, that in international affairs her leadership be on the highest level, that to an order of peace they might best contribute together rather than apart. The trend toward dissociation, completed in Ireland and Burma, satisfied in Pakistan and Ceylon, arrested in India and South Africa, was quickened by the war against the Axis. Yet even for those whose association with Britain is closest, even for Britain herself, these grander world postulates, at once so comfortable and so comforting, can, despite the momentum of the past, no longer be as valid as they were. Never did Commonwealth countries confer and consult with each other more. It is Washington rather than London upon whose initiative or concurrence they now must wait.

Anglo-American concord, if no love match, is one of those *mariages de convenance* which endure by virtue of the deep community of interest on which they repose. For that reason the United States would not dream of replacing Britain at the core of the Commonwealth relationship. As a Commonwealth linchpin she can tender no feasible substitute for that mechanism of unity with liberty which is furnished for all its members—except India—by the constitutional monarchy or, to be exact, the constitutional monarchies under the same crown. Two world wars and Russia's postwar rivalry have taught the United States that friendship with the Britannic realm is a major aspect of American power; that the more power Britain herself possesses in Europe and overseas, the more stability she is afforded through her Commonwealth partnership, the better it is for the entire free world. But this will be so only if the British themselves command the requisite authority, moral as well as political, among Commonwealth colleagues and imperial clients. That it can be done the Britain of the Dunkerque years showed. That it will be done is another question.

The polarization of world power having occurred, it is accentuated by technological, demographic, and strategic factors. There are fewer important counters today on the European chessboard, even as western Europe regains a modicum of strength, than there were yesterday. Before 1914, for example, the Austro-Hungarian monarchy, while riveted to its Hohenzollern ally in Hapsburg quarrels with the czar, was neither German in sovereignty nor were its subject territories pro-Russian in any sense other than the desire to have their Slavonic big brother set them free. In that epoch even Italy was not tied irrevocably to the Triple Alliance, while on Europe's western fringe both France and Britain were in the front rank of world affairs. After the victory of 1918, moreover, the latter were predominant from one end of the Continent to the other—a position they would have held had they stayed united. But centers of intermediate power which could exist in the middle of Europe until Hitler was allowed to wipe out the Little Entente can hardly do so any longer. As far as the Stettin-Trieste line, the Eurasian monolith overawes them all, and it is only that world balance of which the Atlantic Alliance is a prime tool by which Russia's westward expansion has been halted.

Could Britain, so as to ensure economic recovery and for the sake of the common defense, integrate herself in a federal union of western Europe or of non-Soviet Europe as a whole? It is most improbable. In easier days Britain's influence in Europe was nourished by her power overseas, just as the European security thus obtained was the condition for an ever widening range of British activities, political and strategic, imperial and commercial, across the oceans. More, too, than her continental allies—though they also are not self-sufficient—Britain has to buy the bulk of her essential foodstuffs overseas so as to feed a large urban population and to purchase raw materials which, when exported in a finished state, might help her to pay her way. With dollars scarce in the sterling area and until American tariff barriers are lifted, neither she nor other Commonwealth countries can afford to relinquish their preferential tariff arrangements. Indeed whatever happens, Britain might be unenthusiastic about doing this. For under the social nationalism of the Left, her trade abroad, like her economy at home, has been planned, while the protectionist Right in Britain has long deprecated those free trade practices such as she herself once best exemplified.

The danger of falling between two stools, of trying to pursue objectives which are incompatible, will be clear. Before 1939, and above all before 1914, a balance of payments could be reached and a relatively high standard of living maintained in Britain by adding together the visible and invisible items of current account. Among the latter, however, were proceeds accruing from wealth accumulated by earlier generations. The Industrial Revolution began in Britain; and, with her post-Napoleonic mastery of the seas, British enterprise had a head start in furthering world commerce and in developing new lands. But many of the investments thus garnered the British had to liquidate in order to finance themselves during the first World War and then through the opening years of the second; the unrequited sterling balances she has to pay off to India, Egypt, and other countries were incurred by her in fighting a common cause. Yet the advantages she enjoyed in priority of acquisition and as a creditor Power have been receding for over half a century and will never recur. The greatest of seafaring nations, she lost much of her maritime income when a large part of her merchant navy was sunk during the war with the Axis. As the world's leading banker, trader, and investor, Britain did not only serve her own interests. The United States, moreover, has taken over her mission in high politics without emulating her vocation in high finance. And that is one of the chief reasons why the European Recovery Program has had to be energized by subsidies from the American Treasury rather than by the world function, which British trade and investment long performed, of a dominant liberal economy.

The United States, even with her new synthetic industries, is not self-sufficient. Yet she needs world commerce much less than Britain ever did. To earn life-giving dollars, British salesmanship may be induced to make a special bid for a larger fraction of the tariff-girt, American market. But the mass productive power of the United States was so stepped up by the war that in manufactured goods she can overwhelm foreign competition at home and dwarf it abroad almost at will.

Britain may still have important markets in which to compete with others or to receive privileged treatment, shipping to provide, and tourist travel to promote. Outsiders will, however, be reluctant to avail themselves of banking and insurance services that have been collectivized. Socialism, whether it tarries with the Conservatives or moves on with Labour, may yet discover incentives for workers and management as efficacious as any under capitalism; costs might even be lowered and modernized plant installed to improve Britain's productive capacity. But those nations she herself built up have themselves forged industrially to the front. Britain's share of an expanding world economy can never again be proportionately what it once was. And at the moment her task is to hold her own in a competitive world economy that is not expanding.

Under the circumstances can Britain organize a combination of the Brussels Treaty Powers and the countries of the Commonwealth as a Third Force between those two Titans, the United States and Russia? When spokesmen for the Labor and Conservative parties voice the belief that she can, they merely demonstrate how awkward they find it to reconcile themselves to her lesser role on the world stage:

> Perhaps the plaintive numbers flow
> For old, unhappy, far-off things,
> And battles long ago.

On a famous occasion the Emperor William II incurred resentment in Vienna when he thanked his Austro-Hungarian ally for having been "a brilliant second." English-speaking solidarity will not be as robust as the East-West crisis demands unless the United States eschews an alienating if inalienable vice of pontification and the United Kingdom accepts with good grace a reversal in its fortunes which its own self-destructive prewar policies accelerated. For what has changed in Anglo-American cooperation is not its necessity but its order of precedence in common world initiatives, its protocol of power. During the first half-century of their modern friendship—except for the period of American intervention in 1917–1918, the 1919 peacemaking, and the Washington Naval Conference which ensued—Britain occupied a primary and the United States a secondary rank within it. Even so, the strength which was added thereby to our world system the Germans twice underestimated. Today it is Britain herself which occupies a more secondary rank. And while she, too, adds great strength to Anglo-American amity, most of her effective power is derived from the indivisible pool of the West and not from sources of her own which she can, when she likes, wall off from it.

The civilization of the free world would indubitably be safer and with a mass culture less sharply prone to either Russified or Americanized monochromes, richer in color and deeper in content, if Britain, or Britain and France together, could still play their ancient parts. But they cannot. By the same token, lesser Powers might temporarily join with each other in the General Assembly of the United Nations to oppose the ill advised actions of greater ones. On world fundamentals no Third Force can exist for Britain and France independently of the United States.

The preponderance of the West, as headed by her, is not hers alone. Each country of the Commonwealth, Britain among them, must not only contribute its own power to that vast aggregation; some are as likely to do so in conjunction with Washington as London—Canada, at least, refusing to adhere to any additional Third Force which compels her to veer toward the one or the other rather than both. The resources of Latin American and other well disposed nations should be included; any union of non-Soviet Europe, Western or continental, with its colonies and its reviving economic strength, must be enrolled. Even countries in the Orient which cannot side with the West wholeheartedly might realize that their liberty may be favored by our preponderance, just as our preponderance would be facilitated by their good will. In the Mediterranean area as well as in other corners of the earth, the United States shares British defensive interests and in the contingency of war would use British bases. With so interwoven a strategy, with Britain's physical security and daily bread at the mercy of North America, Washington and Ottawa cannot agree that on major issues London may go its own way. But there is no reason why it should, considering what it still can do, good and bad, in the capitals of its overseas allies.

Between the wars, when the United States held herself aloof, the British complained that without her full participation world lawlessness could not be checked nor collective security enforced. This was so over China and perhaps even over Ethiopia; over Europe and over Nazi Germany, Americans could not speak ill of British unwisdom without the finger being pointed at their own. Dying in the United States though not dead, isolationism could not live at all in Britain. But Third-Force notions are those of a group which fain would hunt with the hounds of neutrality while running with unneutral hares. As such they are in vain. To the invalidity of neutrality among Great Powers, all major issues since Versailles have borne witness. Men must choose.

Meanwhile, talk of a world Third Force scarcely generates a fit atmosphere in which to launch the Atlantic Alliance. For any desire manifested in London or Paris to belong and yet not belong must derogate from unity in plan and execution. That a resurgent Germany in Russia's arms might between them match the strength of the

United States herself is plain enough. But, should the latter also be deprived of the close teamwork which the Atlantic Alliance entails, the power surplus which the West still possesses could sink to a bare confrontation of equal power in which Russia would be less sure of defeat and might even gamble on winning; in which so glittering a prize as the conquest of Britain herself seems more within reach. And that being the case, when British public men console themselves with *la recherche du temps perdu* as a projection of the future, their mood of nostalgia should not be misread as a mature statement of policy.

Subsidizing the recovery and underwriting the defense of western Europe, the United States will not be encouraged to persist in good works if her overseas friends seek to exercise an undue measure of detachment from their North American guarantors. Britain was celebrated in Europe as *La Puissance Médiatrice* when she stood in world affairs on her own feet and when, by casting her weight from one side to the other, she could manipulate the course of events. So disjoined a concept of the balance of power was repudiated during the first decade of this century by Lord Lansdowne and Sir Edward Grey as, in addition to the new Anglo-American understanding, they aligned Britain with Japan, with France, and with Russia. Unable to be a free agent then, she is less capable of being one now; and if commitments do not preserve peace they may, at least, prevent submission. For Britain, as the Atlantic Alliance testifies, is herself an integral portion of that world system directed from Washington in whose preponderance resides the main assurance of her own survival.

Within the broad limits delineated by so profound a mutuality of interest there is, however, room for freedom of maneuver. And nowhere has this been more the case than inside the Britannic realm itself. We were handicapped during the Battle of the Atlantic by Ireland's neutrality; abstaining from the Atlantic Pact because of the Anglo-Irish dispute over the northern counties, Ireland as a republic will still be one of its beneficiaries. The Union of South Africa has not seceded from the Commonwealth after all; the new imperial defense preparations in East Africa must serve to enhance her own continental security. More impressive was the manner in which Nehru's India, having achieved her goal of republican dissociation, turned back and gladly accepted an ingenious formula of Commonwealth reassociation. For Sino-Soviet arms are pounding down to her threshold as those of the czar never could in Curzon's day; on her own receptive soil the Communist evangel is afoot. It was therefore to India's national interest not to dissever the web of interdependence—preferential trade, financial, technical, strategic—which had been spun over the years of dependence, but to reaffirm it.

Recognizing the King as head of the Commonwealth, yet renouncing fealty to him, India's membership is a strictly practical one. And as such it is another example of power, acting in this instance as a bond of synthesis, having priority over ideology—over an ideology founded, moreover, in antithesis to it. Behind a lofty façade of unworldly abstractions, India, too, thus walks on the less slippery ground of realism.

This, to be sure, will not hamper her from being leader of the moral forces of Asia. But to win respect on that score she will have to live down the bloodshed and brutalities which attended her partition and which had no foreign aggression, as in Palestine, to bedevil it; the flight of millions from their persecutors, Hindu, Sikh, Moslem, on either side; the state of war between her and Pakistan over Kashmir and Hyderabad; the spiritual arrogance which chides others—a trait usually attributed to unctuous "Anglo-Saxons"—for faults which she also displays. And there is perhaps a hint of this moral pretentiousness when she declares that she will abstain from the East-West contest so as to be able eventually to mediate for peace. For if all took that quasi-isolationist view there would be none to defend freedom, India's as much as any. In the two world wars of the twentieth century the contribution of United India to victory by the West was no trifling one. Today, however, she is so divided at home and so menaced on her frontiers that her didactic fence sitting may, in these years of crisis and until the republic is stronger, be what would best save her from disruption and conquest.

But while this is a more intelligible policy for her than it was for the United States or would be for Britain and France, expediency is not elevated into nobility of principle merely because India has to pursue it.

Canada, Australia, and New Zealand have faltered least in upholding the Commonwealth fellowship and its common allegiance, although in wartime American forces would be more likely than British to operate on their soil. Collectively they thus maintain a historic association, even while between London and Washington each oscillates individually and in varying degrees. For the flexible relationship which evolved within the Commonwealth has been extended to that wider English-speaking community which includes the United States. Nor is the latter grouping more insusceptible to controversy than the former has been. But with Sino-Soviet clouds darkening the East Asian horizon, Australia is modulating her dissent over the American restoration of Japan and talking instead of a Pacific regional pact whose backbone would be American military power; taking a leaf out of Ottawa's book, she now wants her American ties to be as close as her Commonwealth ties. And within the broadest American-Commonwealth framework, Canada, too, may rotate back and forth, up and down. One reason she has stayed out of the inter-American system has been to stress North American and North Atlantic interests while, by steering away from the hemisphere orbit of the United States, she retains more freedom of action. But if the Commonwealth should ever be overweighted by its growing Asiatic membership, if Asiatic considerations should over-influence British foreign policy, Ottawa may gravitate from London to Washington. For between English-speaking members of the Commonwealth, Anglo-American unity in Europe and Asia has become the prerequisite of their own inner Commonwealth unity.

Nor are centripetal factors among so many centrifugal ones, even for Britain, an unmixed blessing. They tend to bolster her diminished world position and her lower status within the Anglo-American fold itself; but because of them, as has often happened, she may have to soft-pedal some special interest of her own. For the time has long passed when at Washington, in the United Nations, or in world councils anywhere, the Commonwealth as such could speak with a single voice. Pressure politics within the fabric of American-Commonwealth friendship are not, however, analogous to the fitful, intermittent dream of a Third Force led by Britain which might mediate between East and West. For that could only take shape by abating our common front. The American-Commonwealth circle, despite internal shifts and differences of a household character, is the rock on which it rests.

Meanwhile, as Anglo-American leadership changes hands, one of its younger partners has come of age. Early in the Hitler war the present writer began to argue that Canada had a new stature which distinguished her from feebler, more inert, or comparatively less productive nations; that, though not of major rank, her position has ceased to be a minor one; that she was what he called a Middle Power—a term which has since entered into common usage and a concept whose functional application was recognized in Article 23 of the United Nations Charter.* For when Britain fought on alone, Canada, with other Commonwealth countries, rushed to her help. Apart from Canada's relative importance as a belligerent and as an air-training center, the output of her factories, mines, fields, and forests was contributed to Britain and the rest of the anti-Axis combine overseas through Mutual Aid, her own form of Lend-Lease; to some of them her postwar gifts and credits have also been generous. During the sterling area's dollar crisis she sat in with Britain and the United States, joined the tripartite arrangements for continuing consultation, and with them, as a leading trader, plumped for a multilateral rather than bilateral system of world commerce.

Not that Canada's boom of the past decade may persist into the next. She is the main customer of the United States and the United Kingdom's chief supplier. Buying twice as much from the United States as she sells to it, Canada also feels the pinch of the world short-

* For a postwar analysis, Lionel Gelber on "Canada's New Stature" in *Foreign Affairs*, New York, January, 1946. For a wartime summary of his Middle Power theory, *Behind the Headlines*, Vol. 4, No. 2, 1944, a pamphlet published by the Canadian Institute of International Affairs.

age in American dollars. Her difficulties diminish as some of her exports to Britain and Europe are financed by dollar grants from the Economic Cooperation Administration; they grow when the United Kingdom itself, becoming agriculturally more self-contained, increases its purchases from sterling bloc countries or deals elsewhere in straight barter. Yet even as these hurdles spring up, new paths are blazed in Canada through recent oil and iron developments; with its immense, untapped natural riches and its high standard of living the Canadian economy is fundamentally sound. And as world power shifts from western Europe to North America, it finds Middle Power Canada standing at the side of her great neighbor as one of the two overseas guarantors of the security of the West.

By signing the Atlantic Treaty she, too, moreover, has taken a new course. "We live in a fireproof house," said one of her spokesmen at Geneva during the long armistice between the wars, "far from inflammable materials." And so in her snug, quasi-isolationism she refused to subscribe to the Locarno Pact and, though a member of the League of Nations, sought to water down Article X of the Covenant. But her 1939 intervention and all that has followed belie the homespun, continental provincialism of those years; once the city of men is in flames, her own dwelling place cannot escape. And because she can now do it in conjunction with her North American associate, she has subscribed, under the Atlantic Pact, to the sort of prior commitment with Britain and western Europe from which she had previously abstained. But in the air-atomic age she is not only more internationally-minded than she was; continental defenses are now also necessary even if overseas barriers do not break down. And, besides, preparations made in common with the United States relieves the latter of any desire to make them alone, to violate Canada's sovereignty when so doing. Politically, Canada protects her national identity against Washington by allying herself with it. Territorially, she also safeguards thereby her national integrity.

Against the danger of a Europe united by conquest, North America has designed its own strategic unity. In 1940, when the Germans swept to the Atlantic, the Permanent Joint Defense Board was set up between Canada and the United States; in 1949, when the East-West schism had become acute, a joint committee for Canadian-American industrial mobilization supplemented this earlier arrangement. Great-circle air routes from the United States to Europe and Asia traverse the soil of Canada; while the climate precludes large-scale land warfare or large-scale bombing forays across the northern polar cap, there might be diversionary raids by single machines, guided missiles, or even infantry detachments from both continents. Against these possibilities a Canadian-American radar warning screen has been projected; in northern defense the air forces of the two countries fly almost as one. With Alaska, the heart of her Arctic operations, the United States communicates by land and air through Canada. For there, where Theodore Roosevelt won his presidential spurs as a power politician, the scene of the last Canadian-American dispute in which the stronger of the two menaced the weaker with war, Alaska today is a rampart of their northern cooperation.* Control of Eurasia by a Russo-German grouping could alter the world equilibrium strategically and industrially. Nor is it inconceivable that its outer rim thus unified might furnish a connected series of jumping-off grounds from which to synchronize attacks on three sides of North America by air.

Indicative of Canada's new status is her share in the atomic-energy venture. She has been devoting herself to scientific research and not to the manufacture of atomic weapons. But if she had merely possessed uranium-bearing ore, she could not have collaborated as she has with the two major English-speaking Powers or have, in this regard, been treated by the United Nations as on a par with the Big Five. And though she has incurred international obligations which might pin her down, Canada's new continental and North Atlantic commitments could also provide her with an unusual freedom to act. A Middle Power in world politics, she is also the one Power which is in the middle of Anglo-American friendship. Eager to reconcile Commonwealth ties with geographical necessities, she has set the coordination of British and American policies as a basic one

* Gelber, *The Rise of Anglo-American Friendship*, pp. 37–58, 136–166.

of her own. And it is significant that the common triune front is maintained when, in the boldest step of her peacetime external affairs, she, too, underwrites the security of the North Atlantic area. But since none of them can now afford to get seriously out of line with its allies, Canada might lift the inhibitions she has imposed on herself, the reticence which her diplomacy often exhibits lest she or the others part company. The British public, at any rate, have over the years somehow been made more aware of the dissent of such sovereign pro-British countries of the Commonwealth as Australia or New Zealand when, in the affairs of the League of Nations or the United Nations, Britain herself has gone amiss. That the survival of Britain and France is of cardinal importance to Canada, her participation from the start in the two German wars abundantly proved; as buyers and sellers, Canada and Britain have large economic interests that are interdependent. But as one of the two overseas signatories of the Atlantic treaty of mutual assistance, Canada is again more likely to come to the rescue of Britain than Britain to her rescue.

Situated by history between the United Kingdom and the United States, the Canadian people are too often content, in the expression of views, to receive from both and yet transmit to neither. The United States thus gets plain talk from all quarters except the one that is closest to her—the one that she does not know as well as she should but that knows her as well as she knows herself. Canadians, chary of political annexation by the United States, once voted against reciprocity in the sphere of commerce and tariffs; strategically that principle is now the order of the day. From combined endeavors in the domain of defense to the joint development of the waters of the St. Lawrence, the destiny of the two North American nations has been merged indissolubly. And while favorable trade relations with the United States and an adequate amount of American dollars are vital to Canada's prosperity, Canada's well-being is essential not only to the business but to the continental and overseas security of the United States herself. Preoccupied with her own growth as a nation, too circumspect to dramatize her greater role, Canada has long been conscious of her need of others. She will rise to her full stature as a

Middle Power when she realizes the degree to which she herself, the resources of her land, and the resourcefulness of her people, are also needed.

The sovereign members of the Commonwealth can all do as they please. In that separate cluster of dependencies from which independent Commonwealth countries emerged, Britain still has the last word. For the British Empire is the mightiest of colonial Powers; to tremors in the colonial world its political seismograph is more sensitive than any other. And these may be twofold. There is first of all the legitimate aspiration to self-government of many subject peoples; there is, secondly, the strategic problem of colonial territories which the East-West contest of power has again aggravated. Britain's world status has owed much to overseas possessions on which the sun was reputed never to set. As she sloughs these off or as they tear themselves away, her strength in international affairs lessens.

The quandary of colonialism is, in terms of the preponderance of the West, a grave one. For through its backing, ideological and material, of sympathetic native forces, the Soviet Union foments unrest within the scattered dependencies of foreign rivals. Compact rather than geographically far-flung, its own empire is as unfree as other portions of the Russian totalitarian police state; beyond his own domestic confines the oppressor can nevertheless pose as patron of the oppressed. And the latter in turn will accept help, just as the West and the Soviet were to make common cause against the Axis, wherever it is proffered. Later on, that very colonial nationalism which has spelled the partial disintegration of empires might ally itself with the West against Russian imperialism. But Russia, through its own Asian expanse, will always have a wider and more direct access than the Powers of the West to the Orient.

Asia for the Asiatics, the sundering of foreign chains, colonial and economic—such are the cries with which Japan and the Soviet Union have each stirred the masses of the Orient against the Occident. That they really meant Asia for the Japanese, or the ascendancy within it of the Russians themselves, is merely to reiterate that, in the struggle for world power, ideas are also counters. Is there time to parry the thrust of Moscow with ideas as potent? Can the industrialization of some colonies, the social reform and development schemes which are forecast for subject peoples at various stages of political growth yet preserve large tracts of the empires of the West? Somehow the leaders of colonial nationalism will have to be convinced that under no other auspices are its chances of liberty as good or its prospects of economic progress better.

Not since the nineteenth century has the United States, often depicted as noncolonial or anticolonial, consistently been either. At first and in the main, her own imperial expansion could be overland and therefore North American; yet she too was to push beyond the water's edge. Her latest economic arrangements with the Philippines demonstrate that even now she has not entirely forfeited the special privileges that went with colonialism; as an apostle of decent relations between white and colored peoples she has much to correct within her own borders. The strength of her associates, moreover, and the vantage points they hold are so essential to the defense of the West that she also benefits from the present distribution of imperial power —that of Britain and France especially—under other allied flags. Not that the *status quo* in colonial empires is satisfactory to her or to many others. The problems of Asia and Africa, while different in origin from the East-West schism, have ineluctably become part of it; if the Occidental contest must shape our world, that in the Orient will be shaped by it. One truth the perpetual crises of the twentieth century have clarified. To liberalize the lands of Asia and Africa can, as in Europe or the Americas, be of little use if the incapacity of the weak in a world of the strong results first in liberty and then only in an exchange of taskmasters.

Though altruism is seldom a motivation in public policy, common interests may well be. Whether capitalist or socialist, much of Britain's world rank and domestic prosperity is founded on her overseas connections; the colonial Powers, led by her, must now persuade all who are free, and all who would be free, that the common welfare can still be a bond between them and their dependencies.

President Truman, in his inaugural address, caught the world's imagination when he proposed that the technological and capital resources of his and other Western countries be employed to spark the development of more backward ones; that what he conceived to be democratic fair-dealing replace the old imperialism. And the Commonwealth, at its Ceylon parley in 1950, sponsored a parallel program of economic aid to Asia and Southeastern Asia. If the West while retiring from Asia does not retrench and, where it stays on—there or in other colonial areas—does so only to alleviate and emancipate, it might outshine Russia ideologically and perhaps even politically. And we shall have shown the Orient that, while its submission would be harmful to us, in the West's preponderance it, too, has a stake.

This does not signify that the two principal English-speaking Powers can in matters of empire, strategy, or foreign trade give each other a blank check. East and West have their ideological quarrel; the socialization of Britain must not furnish a subsidiary one within our own camp. But while the United States has tried to help restore Britain economically, they are, at a time of economic strain, again competitors in world markets. And this competition is sharpened when, as with the Argentine or East-West trade in Europe, the bilateral arrangements of a controlled dollar-starved economy exclude the multilateral dollar-rich commercial practices of one that is not state-directed. Over dealings with Communist China, however, London did not let itself get too far ahead of Washington. Elsewhere, also, there is an Anglo-American contest of power—that frequently unamiable jockeying for position within a mutually indispensable friendship—which proceeds concurrently with the perennial East-West crisis. Neither Britain nor the United States, for example, wants the Russians to obtain the oil of the Middle East, yet each, through its cultivation of Arab rulers and politicians, itches for the lion's share; the one would attain, the other maintain, paramountcy in the region. During the formative stage of the Palestine issue no unity was feasible or, at least, no agreement in which the United States would not also cast honor to the winds while nullifying her own interests and frustrating those of world order itself.

Elsewhere in the Mediterranean the trends have run less discreditably and more intelligently toward a rapprochement. Support by the United States of Greece and of Turkey, the main bastion of the West in the Near East, has been welcome to their British ally. Cyprus, whose nationalists look to Athens and whose Communists to Moscow, may nevertheless be held by Britain and, with Malta, replace Alexandria and Haifa as Anglo-American bases—air, sea, radio. On the disposition of the Italian colonies, London and Washington were at last of the same opinion. Meanwhile, the British protectorate of Cyrenaica gives the Atlantic Allies sea and air bases on the eastern littoral of North Africa with strategic access to centers elsewhere possessed or eyed by the Soviet Union.

As for Italy herself, if she were to go Communist the southeastern frontier of France would be open to an enemy advancing down the Po Valley. Russian power seated on the Italian peninsular boot might cut the Mediterranean in half. The economic assistance she has derived from the European Recovery Program and her signature on the Atlantic Pact demonstrate the strategic importance of Italy and Italian territory in the land, sea, and air defense of the West. But she could not be accepted as our ally and yet be treated as her African and European transgressions have warranted. Moscow would exploit our moral dilemma if we did not let the Italians exploit it themselves. But unlike a revived Germany, with her game of playing off one side against the other, the culture, the religion, the national interests, the basic economic disabilities of Italy, link her with the West and not the East. Many of her sons fought bravely for us in the post-Mussolini phase of the war with the Axis; though notorious as opportunists, many more have since displayed a genuine preference for representative self-government. Their volatile individualism, eclipsed under the bogus Caesarism of the Fascists, could in different ways render both democracy and Communism unworkable. But there is a distinction between the ideological risks which can be taken with a restored Italy and a restored Germany. For Germany's strength may be turned against the West, while Italy is more of a danger when infirm.

Meanwhile, a new emphasis is being put by Britain on her territories in East and Central Africa. For here is an area with a tremendous hinterland which may be defended in the event that the Middle East—or even western Europe—were to become strategically untenable; one which has stupendous natural resources and which, with adequate communications to render them accessible, could maintain a fighting front of its own or assist in the peacetime revival of Britain's domestic economy. Closer unified control, as other rich segments of empire fall away, is mooted; some of it, with self-governing Southern Rhodesia, might even be federated into a single Capricorn Africa—but only if native rights are first safeguarded. Such developments, moreover, might be undertaken by Britain in cooperation with European allies whose African possessions also figure largely in their own domestic well-being—with Portugal, with France, and with Belgium. It is the uranium ore of the Belgian Congo which, like that of the Canadian Arctic, is used by the United States and Britain in nuclear research and in the manufacture of the atomic bomb.

Without British sea power, and then Anglo-American sea and air power, to reinsure them, the African writ of their European allies might not have run for long. Material progress in the Dark Continent is to the interest of the West; financial aid and technical personnel from the United States will therefore be proffered. But the welfare of Africans themselves must come first. In European colonies or in former German mandates all schemes of integration and development should therefore conform to the trusteeship principles of the United Nations. And on that vexatious issue, over South-West Africa, the annexationist Union of South Africa has already whipped up a storm. Yet, from every standpoint, justice here is the best policy. For in Africa, as in Asia, the European governments will have to tread warily lest nonwhite races conclude that against exploitation they can have no recourse other than that which they are told may be found in Moscow's strangulating embrace.

In southeastern Asia the British may be able to retain more of a residue of empire than other colonial Powers among their European allies. But unless its peoples get food, shelter, and freedom, the Sino-Soviet infiltration of Asian nationalism will continue. It may be too late for the French, after incurring military expenditures which neither they nor the British or the Dutch can afford, to have granted Indo-China independence within the French Union; Moscow knows that the more their fighting strength is sapped out there by rebellion and civil war, the more anaemic their key European role in the Atlantic Alliance at home. Though they plan to double its rubber production, the economy of Indo-China has, however, been knit less intimately into the economy of France than that of Malaya has been in Britain's or that of the Dutch East Indies has been in the Netherlands'. To Malaya and to the British in Malaya, the synthetic rubber industry of North America, born out of our war experience, can be nearly as much of a threat as Communist insurrection. For the sale of the rubber and tin of Malaya, together with the trade of Hong Kong, is still Britain's most lucrative source of American dollars—being, as such, a vital element in her economic recovery and therefore in Europe's. With a mixed population of native Malays and Chinese immigrants, her aspirations to freedom, and those of other British dependencies in southeastern Asia, may be expressed through a larger amount of self-government under the crown. From the Britannic realm Burma dissociated herself entirely. But she is so unfit for freedom, so rent by faction, that to preserve her rice export surplus, to protect her strategic raw materials, and to prevent local Communists from taking her into the Sino-Soviet camp, the regionally interested governments of the Commonwealth were constrained to offer her money and arms. For if Burma and Indo-China go Communist, the defenses of Siam and Malaya will totter and India herself may be in jeopardy.

Nor could even the United States of Indonesia, with its great natural riches, remain unaffected. The struggle there with the Dutch has been a microcosm of the whole postwar colonial issue. We ourselves have had the twin objectives of economic recovery and joint defense in western Europe with the Netherlands as an Atlantic Ally; but there was also the certitude that to suppress Asian nationalism would only be to deliver it into the clutches of Moscow. In a world-wide contest of power, we must reconcile our own aims with each other if we are to reconcile others with us. As a bulwark against Sino-Soviet expansion, Asian nationalism may, in its present phase, not be formidable. The Occident must burn no bridges to the Orient which, now or later, can further a common purpose.

Not least among the ironies of Sino-Soviet conjuncture is the changed attitude of the West toward Hong Kong. During the war many believed that the British, who had built it up, should hand that emporium of commerce over to a liberated China; in 1941, under a full Japanese assault from the mainland, its defenses had collapsed. And at Yalta President Roosevelt is reported to have suggested to Generalissimo Stalin that Hong Kong either be ceded to China or internationalized as a free port.* But today the departure of Hong Kong from the ambit of the West would be a matter of concern to the United States, and to all of non-Soviet Asia, no less than to Britain herself. For while colonialism everywhere has much for which to answer, so also may an anticolonialism which, as in Burma, is indiscriminate and too rigidly doctrinaire.

The struggle for freedom would, in other words, be a less baffling one if it were simply a stark, clean-cut confrontation of the hunger for liberty against the insolence of power. For while among subject peoples, wherever they dwell, the immediate confrontation is one of liberty against power, the world picture is that also of power against power, of a perpetual contest in which one side strives to gain and the other to sustain preeminence. Liberty, unbacked by power, might succumb to power unredeemed by liberty. What must justify, and thereby serve, the West's preponderance is an honest effort to harmonize the two.

And that many in the United Kingdom are still not cognizant of this, their protracted feud with Zionism illustrated. For in what has been for the British people and for the United Nations the test case of Palestine, they seemed resolved to dissipate the moral capital Churchill's Britain had so nobly earned. If an entity as vulnerable as

* Sherwood, *Roosevelt and Hopkins*, p. 866.

the British Empire is to survive, it must have the good will of free men everywhere; but the price of greatness is—greatness. In the Middle East the course of Mr. Attlee's government was one of those blunders that are worse than a crime; across the Atlantic, to the dismay of Britain's friends, they stirred up echoes of perfidious Albion which reach back to the American Revolution and which, with the settlement of the Irish and Indian questions, most of us had prayed would be dispelled forever. For here was not only the classic confrontation of liberty against power, but of liberty incarnate filling by itself what proved, contrary to miscalculations in London, a literal power vacuum.

Yet during the generation of Lloyd George, Balfour, and Smuts, both Zionist and British spokesmen had visualized a Jewish national home, or even Jewish statehood, as a bridgehead of liberty and a salient of power for the Britannic realm in the Middle East. When the Attlee-Bevin ministry asked for the advice of the United Nations, they themselves ruled out any such solution. Over vast derelict territories the Arabs had, after 1919, been accorded self-determination by the Allies, although they did little to wrest their own freedom from the Turks—and were to do even less to defend it against the Axis. For their loyal services, unique between 1939–1945 among the peoples of the Middle East, the Jews of Palestine were rewarded with military occupation, with a mandate unilaterally converted against them into a totalitarian police state, with an official terror which, as always in the annals of imperial repression, begat terror. What British military stores and armament, over and above treaty limits, were later to be handed to the States of the Arab League may never be known. But for more than two critical years after the war, when man power was at a premium in Britain's own industrial recovery effort, when her economy was being subsidized by loans, gifts, and assistance from American and Canadian taxpayers, when every man hour wasted and every cent of dollar exchange squandered prolonged her own serious food deficiencies, tens of thousands of men were nevertheless dispatched, hundreds of millions of pounds were yet expended—and precious lives were lost—on a venture as malevolent. as it was barren.

What the soldiers, sailors, and airmen engaged in this sordid campaign were not told, and what the British public overlooked, was that they held Palestine as a trust and not as a colony to be managed by the arbitrary whim of obscure pro-Arab bureaucrats with an adolescent taste for the servile deference of backward races. To secure the establishment of a Jewish national home, to facilitate Jewish immigration and to encourage the close settlement by Jews on state and waste lands—such were stipulations of the League of Nations mandate that had been honored more in the breach than the observance. After the Nazis took office in 1933 and during the war, the United Kingdom admitted to its own hospitable shores thousands of fugitives from the mounting Teutonic blood lust. But not until they had reacquired the mastery of Europe could the Germans organize their continental system of civilian murder factories, human destruction by production-line methods. Yet Jews who got away were, under the Chamberlain government's 1939 White Paper, barred from Palestine, the one country they were entitled by the law of nations to enter, and either sank with their unseaworthy hulks in the waters of the Mediterranean or were caught and reshipped, like trapped animals, at its ports.

Nor did our victory bring freedom to the survivors. Hundreds of thousands of Europeans, stray remnants of six million Jews gassed or incinerated by the Germans, were penned up afterward by the Allies in the charnel houses of their vanquished tormentors, tracked down on the Mediterranean, or piratically hauled off and lawlessly detained behind the barbed wires of Cyprus. And so, too, the Jews of Palestine, the one community which had both the simple humanity and international right to offer their brethren sanctuary, redoubled their resistance to Mr. Bevin's gross edicts. Tragic for them, it was nevertheless sad as well for Britain when she allowed glory won during the war against Hitler to be tarnished by the degradation of war against his chief victims.

Nor will it do to point to the declaration of independence by

India and Burma, the membership of Pakistan, Ceylon, and India in the Commonwealth, as acts which even up the moral score. These were historic events. They were not, however, gifts of liberty which Whitehall in its largesse could tender or withhold at will. In the rebellious subcontinent of India, at any rate, they were concessions of a kind which had long been denied by force and which, against force, could not be denied one moment longer. When Gandhi and Jinnah extorted them from Britain, she was exhausted by the conflict of 1939–1945, immersed in Bevin's sterile war against helpless refugees and Zionist idealism, threatened with insurrection in Malaya, and buoyed up economically by the United States—a Power sympathetic to India's revolution. Only in Palestine was Britain at first not constrained to surrender to the inevitable; only there could she still have exercised freedom of choice. For as late as 1947 she might have contrived a solution compatible with both imperial interests and Zionist statehood—air, sea-base, or other facilities being granted in Palestine, as elsewhere, by one government to another if their quarrel is healed in time. Bad morally, the decision she made was as incompetent strategically. For Palestine revealed what India concealed, that Bevin's Britain neither understood the limits of power nor the claims of that liberty which might have merged with power and transfigured it.

As the age-old intersection of Europe, Asia, and Africa, and because of its ready access to that artery of empire the Suez Canal, Palestine once ranked high in British strategy. Lately it has done so less than it did. From Napoleon to Hitler, British sea power, with the control first of Gibraltar and then of Suez, had blockaded in Europe or contained within the Mediterranean every European conqueror bent on world conquest. Today Russia alone is expanding in the Orient; and, as the British Empire contracts, there is none to interpose a stout territorial barrier between her and Suez—if she does not circumvent it and the usual southward routes entirely. East Africa, remote and impenetrable, has therefore become a new foundation of British power—the second line of a Mediterranean land defense whose first line is Cyrenaica and the Persian Gulf. But if such are the trends, there was no necessity to cheat Israel out of her meager space so as to prop up the empty sub-Ruritanian desert "monarchy" of Jordan. Nor should it be forgotten that that British vassalage is a land which was carved in the first place from mandated Palestine and thus taken from the mandate area to which Jewish homeland provisions applied.

But be that as it may, Israel, in her war for freedom, was quick to puncture Whitehall's iridescent bubble of Arab armies as a regional bulwark between Russia and the West or as reliable watchdogs of oil pipelines in the Middle East. She did this, moreover, by improvising an army of her own out of the Jewish Palestine underground and did it under fire. The General Assembly of the United Nations had, in November, 1947, authorized the prior establishment of defense forces as the mandate dissolved and before partition was accomplished. As though to foil that recommendation, an Anglo-American blockade and embargo was nevertheless clamped down almost at once. Against the Army of Israel the cease-fire regulations of the Security Council were later also to choke off supplies, leaving the aggressors, the invading Arab regular armies, with their gradually acquired stockpiles and any Anglo-American material the British in the Middle East were surreptitiously disposed to provide. All belligerents purchased arms in eastern Europe. But only one—as with countries of the West who had consorted with Russia against Axis aggressors—was fighting for its life. In August, 1949, moreover, all restrictions were lifted as Arab states, preparing to avenge their defeat, obtained fresh military stores. Arms were thus withheld by the Powers from those who, in their hour of jeopardy, were entitled to them, but made openly available again to the aggressors when they girded for a renewal of the attack.

The Arab League was one of the most brazen frauds of modern politics. Yet corrupt feudal potentates and venal politicians of land-satiated Arab countries, with off-stage promptings in a variety of British accents, levied blackmail in the chancelleries and at Lake Success as if they could be deemed a serious power factor and as if, were they shunned by the West, they could risk their own necks by aligning themselves with Russian Communism. Nor would Arab states permanently forego American oil revenues because, on the Palestine issue, President Truman might be prodded spasmodically or even completely out of Mr. Bevin's overstuffed pocket. The fact is that oil areas in the region of the Persian Gulf, the nerve center of current Anglo-American strategy in the Middle East, will, like the Moslem zone of North Africa, be dominated by Great Powers that are there first and stay there longest. So as to ensure safe passage of tankers up and down the Mediterranean, we have Gibraltar and other Allied bases. But to obviate the danger of Arab oil falling into the hands of Moscow, the West should have called an early halt to drilling wells which, undestroyed, the Soviet might seize. In the Orient the vertiginous development of oil fields which the Russians could take over; in the Occident a headlong rush to restore a federally unified industrial Germany with which Moscow might become allied —it is curious how some Anglo-American policies might, in fact, lure Russia on when they are supposed to hold her at bay.

In October, 1947, Britain announced that she would relinquish her League of Nations mandate and subsequently gave assurances that what the General Assembly recommended to replace it would not be opposed. But the golden opportunity which the Attlee-Bevin government then had to extricate themselves from the Palestine embroglio passed. British quarters had not been left in the dark about the ill effects on Anglo-American relations of sticking to their former course. A cold, devious, implacable endeavor, despite their solemn pledges to abstain, still went on behind the scenes in the United Nations and in world chancelleries, at sea, in the air, and on land, to obstruct the creation of the Jewish state which the General Assembly proposed; to bring it to its knees; to rob Israel of strategic frontiers, such as the British Empire sought for itself, after attack by its enemies, in peace settlements being negotiated; or so to mutilate its twice-diminished area that Israel would neither be territorially viable nor capable of ministering to hounded kinsmen who could dwell no longer in the slaughterhouse of Europe nor among their persecutors in Moslem countries. Broken promises were still the fate of the Land of Promise. And in the end the puppet states of the Arab League, other than Jordan, were even more hostile to Britain than the Republic of Israel which, on their behalf, she had striven to obliterate. Portentous for the West, above all, was the fact that British statesmanship, regaining under Churchill the solvency it had lost under MacDonald, Baldwin, and Chamberlain, was bankrupt again.

The Attlee-Bevin government, with the aid of the Security Council, debarred the General Assembly from establishing in Palestine its prescribed transitional authority. During 1948 the 1947 Plan of Partition had therefore to be implemented, as far as possible, in the teeth of foreign invasion by the nascent Republic of Israel itself. Thumbing its nose at the decision it had requested from the General Assembly, the mandatory Power, while still suzerain, had almost at once opened the frontiers of the country to armed Arab "irregulars" who laid siege to Jerusalem. Yet as a feature of the United Nations partition scheme, for whose full pre-Israel implementation the Jewish Agency for Palestine pleaded, Jerusalem would have been internationalized. Surrounded by territory which had been allocated to a proposed Arab Palestinian state, and though it is inhabited mainly by Jews, Jerusalem was to be a United Nations responsibility; and so the war against Jerusalem, more even than the war against Israel, was war against and within the world organization itself. The small Old City fell. And when the 100,000 beleaguered Israelis of Jerusalem's New City withstood an assault by Egypt and Jordan, comparable in harm to the Nazi blitz on London, they were fighting native janissaries, many of whom were paid, trained, supplied, armed, munitioned, officered, and commanded by a Great Power which, with the help of other freedom-loving peoples, had itself scarcely recovered from a tyrant's onslaught.

For the British mercenaries of Jordan and Iraq were, in Israel's war of independence, to be what the Hessians of George III had been in America's. Richard Coeur de Lion would turn over in his grave could he but learn that, in what preens itself on being a more enlightened age, the latter-day servants of an English crown might conspire with the infidel to damage or raze the sacred shrines, Christian and Jewish alike, of the Holy City. In those months of grace, however, the conscience of the West was mute as Mr. Bevin, a Crusader in reverse, sweated to make all of Jerusalem the monopoly of an alien Moslem invader. The principle of internationalization was only recalled later when the besieged Israelis, who alone had preserved it, refused to rely any longer on unenforced and unenforceable United Nations projects which left them, men, women, and children, to starve and die under Anglo-Arab guns. For the fate of their slaughtered kinsmen in Hitler's Europe had taught them to behave at last like that animal in La Rochefoucauld which was so wicked that, when attacked, it defended itself.

The moralist in politics is, as Machiavelli intimated long ago, not seldom forlorn. But an ethical realism, power that is moral, may, it has been argued in these pages, yet build a better world. To this contention was, however, imparted a harsh ironic twist by the lurid contrast between the two most spectacular sieges, that of Berlin and that of Jerusalem, of the postwar epoch; one which the acid pens of Aristophanes, Swift, and Voltaire would have been perplexed to depict and over which Mephistopheles at his wryest must have cast his spell. For Berlin, whose rafters had rung with Germanic cheers for the pagan enemies of Christendom, suddenly was converted into a special object of the West's charity and solicitude; Jerusalem, whose common defense should have been a spiritual aim of the civilized West no less than a political right of its battered inhabitants, was abandoned simultaneously to war and desecration. And while in Berlin British power helped succor millions of recent Nazis who had toiled to bring Britain low, it backed at Jerusalem the lawless besiegers rather than the suffering besieged. Nor did the sequel clear so fetid an atmosphere. For while praise was lavished on Berliners when they endured Muscovite discomforts, the Israelis of Jerusalem, by winning freedom for themselves and by themselves, received no such commendation.

Nevertheless, it may not have been on them but on the United Nations itself that Britain and her Middle Eastern satellites inflicted their most crippling blows. The Security Council, before whom and without reproach Arab representatives shrilly avowed their bellicose designs, is directed by the Charter to determine the existence of any threat to the peace, breach of the peace, or act of aggression. Though the American delegate spoke once of Arab aggression, the Council itself, when Israel and Jerusalem were attacked on land and from the air, flouted this precise injunction. Anglo-Arab armies, operating beyond their frontiers, were instead protected month after month against ejection by the Israeli defenders and crystallized in advance positions on terrain other than their own as all belligerents were ordered to cease fire—a tragicomic ritual which to the Security Council became more sacrosanct than its prime and inescapable duty under the Charter to decide what should be done to restore international peace and security. In episodes other than Palestine, the East-West contest, or considerations arising from it, has made the Security Council a lath painted to look like iron. Without any such excuse here, its behavior was all the more inexcusable. The upshot is, as it was bound to be, that on other issues it does not come into court with clean hands. Not that the Security Council is a court. But moral is as moral does—a maxim upon which Mr. Bevin's ill assorted majority at the Council table might well have pondered at the start.

A firm voice in Washington could have brought London to its senses. Until very late, however, that was lacking. Whitehall thus made the most of the administration's reluctance to superimpose an Anglo-American squabble on that East-West crisis with which the United States is, in the main, preoccupied. Yet Britain can do without Anglo-American solidarity as little, or even less, than the United States; and if when American diplomacy should have been rapping London over the knuckles, Mr. Bevin year after year could induce demoralizing vacillation in high places on the Potomac, it was because not all there felt that his objectives were as vile as his methods. Yet Mr. Bevin and his coadjutors, though they tried, could not move the problem into the center of East-West embitterment. In November, 1947, when it voted for partition and thus for Zionist statehood, the General Assembly's two-thirds majority would not have been obtained without the influence of President Truman in the White House; despite intermediate divagations the

United States and Russia have stood nearer together on this than on any other major contemporary problem. But there were factions within and below the American cabinet which did not grasp how imperative it is for the leadership of the West to repose on a record more unsullied than that of the East. Yet if they had, the United States, through the convergence on this key issue of Russian and American policies, might have saved the United Nations from pusillanimity and the Security Council from itself.

The Soviet bloc, like most of the West, recognized the case for Jewish statehood in Palestine. But for Zionist activities in Russia the penalty is still what it always has been, banishment to Siberia; as is everyone else, the Jews there are trapped, while from other eastern European countries—those haunts of the pogrom and mass source for the German crematories—emigration to Israel has periodically been forbidden. Orphaned children and middle-class survivors of Nazism who now feared imprisonment behind the Iron Curtain were, as they fled to their Mediterranean haven, stigmatized nevertheless by the Goebbels brush of Mr. Bevin and his minions as pro-Communist. Nor does it suffice to explain this sickening, mean-spirited quarrel in terms of the postwar Soviet factor. As long ago as 1937, Britain's own Royal Commission, headed by Lord Peel and counseled by Sir Reginald Coupland, did not only propose the principle of partition which Mr. Bevin later did his utmost to torpedo. It denounced the churlish manner in which British officials were discharging their obligations to the Jews under the mandate at a time when the German shadow lay heavier than the Russian.

The fact is that it was Britain herself who introduced the Soviet Union into Palestinian affairs. It will be remembered how the General Staff of imperial Germany transported Lenin back to revolutionary Russia and thus engineered the spread of Bolshevism. When the Attlee-Bevin government rejected the direct negotiation of a reasonable agreement with the Jewish Agency for Palestine and asked the United Nations to deliberate on the topic of Palestine, they themselves were inviting Communist Russia, as one of its two chief members, to have a say on the future of a Middle Eastern zone where

Anglo-American interests were uppermost. They also slammed the door thereby on any settlement which might have accorded Britain strategic rights in Palestine not as easily available elsewhere. To woo Israel, the Soviet Union had, on this issue, merely to conform to the Charter and the unamended 1947 partition resolution of the General Assembly. Yet neither the ineptitudes of Washington and Paris nor the malice of London could, to the detriment of the West, drive that young, sorely tried social democracy into Moscow's arms. Instead, if the valleys of the Jordan, the Tigris, and the Euphrates are, on the pattern of the Tennessee Valley Authority, ever reclaimed to their ancient fertility, it is the trained mind and Western techniques of modern Israel which can best assist the entire region to hold its own.

On the Palestine question it was, then, not the Security Council but the more widely representative General Assembly which set creative precedents. It adopted the idea of partition as suggested by its own committee of inquiry and it refused afterward to revise its considered judgment; cold feet in Washington and hot heads in London could not induce a demeaning somersault. The Security Council and the Trusteeship Council—the first in general and the second over Jerusalem—did more, however, than shelve the onus of implementing the decision of the General Assembly. When the Security Council was subsequently remiss in pronouncing on the issue of aggression, it was delinquent in that peace-keeping task which is its *raison d'être*. Like Bismarck at the Congress of Berlin, the General Assembly's two subsidiary organs of mediation and con-ciliation (and not any of the Security Council's) have, as honest brokers, rendered service in bringing the belligerents together. But this is no new function in diplomacy. We did not organize the United Nations to be merely a convenient mechanism for good offices such as President Theodore Roosevelt tendered under the politically more difficult circumstances of the Russo-Japanese War. What would justify its mission in this respect is not to facilitate the end of hostilities after the struggle had run its course, but to nip war in the bud at the outset.

Israel, having won, wanted to be sidetracked no longer from

her historic enterprise of national resurrection. Conversely, Arab aggressors would accept any neutral medium through which they might save face and perhaps chivvy out of negotiation a little of what they failed to get by unrebuked invasion. The guns were silenced and blessed is the peacemaker. But still more blessed is the chief business of the United Nations which is, where possible, to preserve peace before it is broken. If the Security Council could not do its job against a miserable Anglo-Arab cabal, it can do it nowhere, and other instrumentalities are bound to rate above it. Only a pathetic need for a major success would account for inflated claims of triumph by the United Nations in a sphere where it had few and for overlooking the fact that while Israel owes much to principles enunciated by the General Assembly, it was by the valor of Israel alone that those principles were vindicated.

Nor could the United Nations insist that Israel, though faithful to its spirit, abide by the letter of a partition resolution which the world organization itself did not enforce. From the wanton Anglo-Arab war for power, the harassed new state learned that, on a smaller scale, it, too, may only have peace by power. Does Israel, seeking less undefendable frontiers, annex territory beyond the absurd patchwork originally allotted, lest it be used by the same unpacified aggressors to throttle her existence? If that is the right of conquest, so is every inch—trusteeships and strategic trusteeships, rectification of boundaries, dominant interests—yielded to us, the West no less than the East, by the Japanese, the Germans, and the Italians. Nor is the United Nations safe from danger. For it will turn all its principles upside down if attackers are rewarded at the expense of the attacked —particularly where the latter had not even been overcome. Yet that is what the two proposals on Jerusalem of its mediator, Count Bernadotte, would have accomplished. And in December, 1949, the General Assembly cast a shadow on its own good record when it revived an obsolete and thoroughly undemocratic scheme for Jerusalem's internationalization—a step which exasperated the Israelis into acknowledging the New City as the ancient capital of their modern State.

And it was as an aspect of her territorial as well as her security problem that Israel dealt with the predicament of Palestinian Arab refugees. These had been stampeded into flight by the Charter-breaking Arab states. And while the latter had funds to wage war and, as Egypt and Syria have now done, to increase their military budget for renewing the struggle, they at first had little room and less money for the resettlement of dupes whose well-being was the pretext for aggression. The callousness with which Arab states treated them was, curiously enough, duplicated in that accorded their own Nazi *Volksdeutsch* from elsewhere in Europe by the postwar Germans. Israel, with her tiny expanse, is, on the other hand, the only country anywhere which may take care of fellow Jews crowding in from the hellholes of Europe and Islam. The liberal treatment her loyal Arab minority has received ranks her, nevertheless, with the best of mixed democracies, the Canadian, the Swiss; she also has offered to repatriate a fair share of those who left her in her hour of trial. But a world that was unconcerned over the sanguinary excesses which, during the partition of India and Pakistan, hurled millions of Hindus and Moslems from hearth and home, was strangely concerned to narrow further the minute space of Israel; to burden her with an over-impressionable, self-exiled fifth column when hostilities might yet be resumed. And this also at a time when reparations are canceled and billions are poured by the West into the restoration of Axis lands while the cost of rehabilitating the pitiful survivors of Nazism's principal victim is laid on private Jewish philanthropy and on the Israelis themselves with the enemy still at their gates. For if Israelis do not prove to be their brother's keeper, nobody else will.

Topsy-turvy throughout, the epic of Israel was, with the exodus of the invading Egyptians, an inversion of the Bible story to which their own protean British ally is indebted. For Britain inadvertently had hedged her bets; whatever happened she could lose neither way. With the victory of foreign Arab states in Palestine she might, through Jordan and Iraq, have flaunted in her cap the tawdriest of feathers; more than this could have done, the defeat of Egypt, the predominant Arab state, has none the less improved the British power position in North and East Africa. The Egyptians, whose defensive value against Russia—as against the Axis—had been exposed as a bad joke, might even be rearmed for Anglo-Arab vengeance against Israel. Before the fate of the Italian colonies had been decided, Britain, which opposed partition in Palestine and acceded to it in India, could now, with her highly selective pro-Arabism, impose it on Libya. Elsewhere Pan-Arabs were enraged. Yet Egypt, on whose military infirmities the outnumbered, underequipped Israelis had thrown the spotlight, had to accept without a whimper the establishment in Cyrenaica, on her western frontier, of yet another fulcrum of British pressure. The British garrison and British aircraft stationed in the Suez Canal Zone might as a result be moved, or the whole blood-soaked dispute be settled at Cairo more as London desires. And the same was true of the British grip on the Anglo-Egyptian Sudan, whose eventual independence would still be harnessed as an important adjunct of a Middle Eastern strategy based on East Africa. The one item of advantage, if they strike a new bargain, which Egypt possesses is her stubborn treaty violation of Suez Canal rules. For Britain incurs a further and quite needless expenditure of dollars as her own ally of the Palestine war prevents the passage of crude oil to the Haifa refinery. It is a cautionary tale. For only those who pour oil on troubled waters may be free to ship it by the same route.

In the end, what during the Palestine fiasco disheartened the friends of the British people was not that they were worse than others but that they had revealed themselves to be no better. Before 1939, German, Japanese, and Italian apologists would argue that what they had done or were going to do was only what the British Empire or even the United States herself had done in their years of imperial expansion. But whatever we did then was at least consonant with the political ethics of the time; and afterward many, though not all, centers of power thus acquired were revamped through Anglo-American concepts of liberty alien to the Germans, the Japanese, or the Italians. The League of Nations, the inter-American system, a plethora of prewar and postwar pacts, the United Nations itself, are tokens of what is designed to be a new ethic of international affairs mitigating and redirecting the concurrent struggle for global power. And it is because Russia has been paying lip service to the one while pressing relentlessly on with the other that so deep a rift exists between East and West. But now the British people themselves, who were supposed to be in the van of world order, have exhibited over Palestine the same sort of dichotomy between word and deed or, at any rate, were indifferent when their ministers spat upon the new ethic and distorted it to serve an old one.

They really cannot behave as though between wars nothing had changed—between, that is, their eighteenth century War of Jenkins's Ear and their twentieth century war for Bevin's ire. Yet where in Britain during the postwar period was that crowning glory of her public life, that spirit among poets and legislators, among men of thought and men of action, which, decade after decade—from the American Revolution to Zionism itself—took up the cause of freedom with ardor and with what Burke called magnanimity? That some Jews resisted violence with violence is no more extraordinary than that for almost two centuries other peoples, inside and outside the Empire, have been doing the same; to such resistance Britain owes her own parliamentary democracy and the free Commonwealth. What did seem remarkable there was the aftermath of mingled anti-Semitism and apathy, though that most civilized of countries would have been ashamed in any previous episode of the sort to disclose so drab an antipathy—one which is embedded so corrosively in the primitive subconscious of the West and to which Zionism itself has been the counterforce.

Before the war, when Britain herself was slipping down the fatal slope of appeasement, her kindness toward Jewish refugees from the Nazi state was commensurate with her own generous traditions. But after the war displaced persons in occupied Germany, waiting in despair for the doors of Palestine or the New World to be opened, encountered an anti-Semitism in the camp administration of the British Zone which was a rancid backwash from the Anglo-Zionist imbroglio. And quite as inconceivable during the past century is the fact that, from Cyrenaica to Aden, Arab territories under direct

British control have witnessed savage postwar pogroms, czarist style, which the authorities did nothing to avert and for which no indemnification has been offered. All this has occurred, moreover, in a sphere where Don Pacífico, a Jew, Greek by residence but British by citizenship, had fired Palmerston to blazon forth the proud, if intemperate, doctrine of *civis Romanus sum*. It befell Jews on that highroad of empire where the Jew Disraeli, purchasing for Britain (with Rothschild help) her Suez Canal shares and enthroning Victoria as Empress of India, brought Britain to the summit of her fortunes in the Orient and her grandeur in the world.

But it was not only over their country's history that the Attlee-Bevin vendetta would slur. Absent, too, was that sporting instinct which in more spacious, and therefore more chivalrous, days must have applauded a smaller antagonist, David against Goliath, who battled so gamely with all the odds against him; that code of gentlemen which evinced disdain for any of their own who, on or off the playing field, went in for the tactics of the cad and the practice of the bully. And even when she needed friends less, a mature democracy such as Britain's would have subjected herself at once to alarmed self-scrutiny over the pronounced disparities between her policies on the Palestine question and those in the General Assembly of the entire English-speaking world overseas—those not only of the United States but, in the Commonwealth, those also of Canada, of Australia, of New Zealand, and of South Africa.

That a deterioration in British public life has supervened will be evident to any who, discerning all that Mr. Bevin was able to do with impunity, recollect how for activities at Geneva, by comparison infinitely more innocuous, Sir John Simon lost favor and Sir Samuel Hoare had instantaneously to resign. And while Mr. Bevin, a professional politician himself, disparaged President Truman's attitude as the concern of a politician for his electors (as if this were not his legitimate business in a representative democracy), it can only have been Mr. Bevin's own mass vote-catching appeal which allowed him to intimidate a cabinet so cynically at variance with its own pro-Zionist electoral pledges. To protests—sorrowing, indignant, or both

—from proven friends abroad, they or their servitors reacted with a humorless pharisaism reminiscent of the Baldwin-Chamberlain period.

Not that there was self-righteousness everywhere over an unrighteous cause. Significant, in the light of imperial and strategic rationalizations circulated by Downing Street, is the fact that against them the two most imperially-minded of Britain's elder statesmen, Mr. Churchill and Mr. Amery, continued to be staunch in their Anglo-Zionist sympathies—together, in the Center, on the Left, and on the Right, with a handful of journalists, publicists, and other public men. Yet for more than three wasted and wasteful years they were but voices crying in the wilderness until a power crisis within the Anglo-American grouping—however disguised or denied—aroused Parliament and, at the behest of the White House, compelled Britain to curb the power she was exercising against Israel. If liberty prevailed against power, power yielded to greater power so that the simple decencies could be preserved.

No doubt the humiliation the British people thus brought upon themselves (and upon those of us who, in their hours of peril, have been their friends) was the upshot of war fatigue, of nerves strained and cities wrecked, and of unrelieved postwar austerities. During the Battle of Britain she alone, backed by her empire and the countries of the Commonwealth, had stood up to the fury of Hitler and Mussolini; hers, moreover, remained a maximum effort throughout. And afterward the endeavor to synchronize industrial recovery with socio-economic change coincided with that harrowing export-import, dollar-sterling crisis which makes her interminably dependent on the bounty of North America. A gallant hard-won victory over the Axis which is yet for her a long-range defeat, financial insecurity coupled with shrinkage in world stature—these have not conduced to the relaxed mood of the good loser. Nor has American support, while a boon, also been a balm; among poor relations jealousy, masked by a false and discreet humility, is more apt than affection to be the guerdon of any interfering, high-handed, thoroughly well intentioned benefactor. It is human enough for the British, disregard-

ing how much of their postwar plight is due to their own prewar im-
policy, to lay the blame elsewhere; to bristle nowadays, whenever
they take stock, with resentments. Only in the revolt of Israel could
they find a safe outlet—the immemorial outlet for the ignorance and
rancor, the fears and frustrations of Western man—through which
to vent their spleen.

Refugees fleeing the poisoned earth of Europe, Israelis sweetening
with their lifeblood the arid soil of their ancient forebears, were
thus the handiest of scapegoats. And they were scapegoats who in-
furiated all the more as they renounced the passive, cheek-turning
role assigned millennially to the Eternal Jew; who, dying and yet
deathless, fought on the rampart of audacity with the secret weapon
of an indestructible faith. Perhaps, in brief, the Israelis were whip-
ping boys for an empire elsewhere in retreat and a Great Power
reluctant to admit that it ranks no longer among the most powerful.
The recessional of Kipling's late-Victorian forebodings was, after all,
in the domain not only of things seen but of things unseen:

> Far-called, our navies melt away;
>   On dune and headland sinks the fire:
> Lo, all our pomp of yesterday
>   Is one with Nineveh and Tyre!
> Judge of the Nations, spare us yet,
> Lest we forget—lest we forget!

Though the Bevins and the Attlees change their tune or even
vanish from the scene, the fact that Bevinism as a state of mind
could for so long a period become the mind of the State demonstrated
that Britain had yet to adjust herself to realities. For the civilization
of the West and for its world preponderance, a strong Britain is
needed. Free peoples cannot, however, work well with her or assist
her spontaneously—their combined unity must suffer—if her conduct
is not only erroneous but unworthy. For to maintain in the world a
balance of power we shall, in our behavior, have first to retain the
power of balance.

What kind of Britain, then, is emerging? Immersed in a revolution of world power and world strategy, she has also been under-

going a socio-economic one of her own. Can Socialism be established without coercion? Attempting to answer that question in the affirmative, the Labor party has done much which the Conservatives will not revoke—even if the eggs could be unscrambled; the challenge, though in opposite directions, is one that has gone out to the socially modified capitalism of North America as well as to the Communist dictatorship of the Soviet Union. Yet the effect, even without nationalization, of the world decrease in Britain's wealth would itself be revolutionary. The leveling down of privileged classes, the leveling-up of others, may result in a more egalitarian society. But as the former dwindle, there might disappear with them a culture of leisure whose patronage of talent, whose habits of civic responsibility, fixed a pattern of distinction in her public life. In the past, and Marxian determinism apart, it was often communities which throve commercially that were creative in art or literature: Periclean Athens, Renaissance Italy, seventeenth century Holland, Elizabethan and Victorian England. So also the high income and wide opportunities which world power furnished long sustained in Britain herself a structure of affairs which fostered leadership and did so in a fashion which was hers alone.

The breadth of views and ease of life which thus flourished may have been founded on a domestic and imperial order of plenty for the few and want for the many. Yet it derived also from her island position which had allowed Britain to be of Europe but not in it; to express her militarism through sea power and colonial wars across the surface of the globe rather than behind her own, or over adjacent, frontiers; to expand out of sight and out of mind where she could be as daring or as domineering as she pleased, while among her complacent upper and middle strata there was only the harsh condition of industrial workers to disturb the even tenor of their ways. Unlike the Germans or the Russians, the immunity of the British to invasion enabled their disciplines to be of the self rather than the state. Autocracy not being for them, neither was absolutism in doctrine—not even that libertarian absolutism which sprang up in France from land power tempered by a heritage of freedom and a tradition of logic. But with the advent of the air-atomic age, Britain is immune no longer. Inroads on her pattern of liberty may be harder to avoid.

At any rate a strategic revolution calling for more home preparedness, if it is not to put her at the mercy of events, coincides with a socio-economic revolution which, while an event of mercy to some, is of a disquieting, semiauthoritarian nature to others. Nor as the social pyramid is flattened out does it rid itself only of an aristocracy at the top. Fitting into the hierarchy of caste, accepting and promoting its values, going down the economic scale as it goes down, has been the large middle class, with its gifts of achievement and replenishment in intellectual and artistic, in professional and scientific pursuits, in the business and governance of an empire. And while this upper- and middle-class nexus bred smugness and snobberies as well as liberality, they were trivial defects as compared with the ferocities of intolerance which totalitarian societies generate in order to feel secure; or even beside the more subtly regimenting impatience of the mass with individuality which all equalitarian societies—pioneer capitalist as well as burgeoning socialist—tend to reflect. For there are many freedoms, and some are relinquished as others are attained. But standardization of opinion, uniformity of thought, dead levels of ingrown mediocrity—it is not for these that the world, until now, has looked to Britain. For her strength, though concrete, could never be epitomized on any mere chart of statistics. In the Commonwealth, among the English-speaking peoples and free men everywhere, her prestige and her capacity to lead, by herself or with others, stemmed also from great imponderables. Will the new social order of the United Kingdom still be their repository? For as the East-West contest grinds on, and as we compute our planetary assets, elements such as these cannot be omitted from the reckoning.

"To govern," said Pascal, "is to foresee." The influence of Britain has meant so much to civilization that we cannot overestimate the epochal gravity of her having entered a world war and stepped from it—though blessed by a saving Churchillian interlude in her authentic tradition—under the auspices, first of the Right and then of the Left, of the second-rate. Does this imply that her performance should always have been better than that of other Great Powers? It does. Yet this discrimination arises from no lack of esteem, but from the very circumstances under which Britain herself has lived, moved, and had her being.

When she was at the apex of affairs, the solidity and stability of her world position obscured the skill tirelessly exerted to keep her there. For while her power was large, and though a surplus of power piled up which permitted a fair margin of error, even that could not be mismanaged with too profligate a hand. And now in leaner times she has no power to spare; the range of permissible error shrinks; the degree of skill demanded of Britain's rulers alone increases—and with no visible reserve to supply the deficiency.

The United States and Russia are, in this respect, more fortunately situated than she is. They and their statesmen can, therefore, get away with much which Britain herself once could, but can no longer, afford. For the difference between them is the difference between land and sea. Territorial coherence gives logic to geography that the eye may grasp at a glance; maritime dispersal is a more subtle, less prodigal, residuum of history which only the mind can recollect. Where Russia and the United States have expanded on inner lines, Britain has had to function on outer and extended ones. The imperial strength of the first two has thus appeared to be a natural phenomenon; that of the latter seems artificial. Not that, where constructive, this has lessened its value. It was the far-flung, essentially artificial, man-made character of Britain's power (naval and colonial, commercial and industrial, financial and diplomatic) which sheltered her own, and the New World's, ideological experiments in constitutional democracy; which, from Napoleon I to William II, was the vigilant sentinel of their unmolested material growth. For, at their best, the Empire she possesses and the Commonwealth which revolves around her have been political achievements of the first magnitude. But while to hold together the natural no exceptional proficiency is required, for the artificial nothing less may suffice.

In one of his less admired *cris de cœur* Winston Churchill declared that he did not become the King's First Minister in order to liquidate the British Empire. Yet what else could he have said? Consider an American utterance in the same vein. What if Mr. Roosevelt or Mr. Truman had proclaimed that all imperial American territories—other than the distant, more developed and long-pledged Philippines—must operate under their own steam? Statehood in the Union cannot expunge the colonial origins of Alaska and Hawaii. What if they, the Virgin Islands, Puerto Rico, the Panama Canal Zone, with all lesser points of vantage in the Pacific and the Atlantic, had, under an ideological impulse, ever been set loose? On American power, and therefore on the security of the free world, the repercussions of this would have been catastrophic. So also with Britain and the joint defense of the West—while a self-centered and unbending power at the expense of liberty must be disastrous, too fluid a liberty at the expense of power might not profit liberty itself. For a century the Britannic realm has been riven, reinforced by the Commonwealth which it bred, and then assailed again by that colonial struggle between liberty and power which the genesis of the United States adumbrated. And now in Britain's parlous condition for her to deny liberty by force would be to expend and therefore lose strength. To grant it may also be to lose strength—but with the chance that not all will be lost, that much may be conserved.

For where each concedes in the common interest, there might be some pragmatic accommodation between liberty and power. But empire that is empiric is not just a problem of bases and colonies strategically well placed in the four corners of the earth. It is even more, in terms of Anglo-American friendship and the Atlantic Alliance, one of Britain's global status. For if, by a controlled economy at home or by an uncontrolled wholesale abolition of empire overseas, she were divested of the power to bolster her world rank, she would cease to be a world center. Designed by Nature to be another Ireland rather than a modern Rome, the small island of Britain could not be impoverished and still sustain her large population—a determinant factor among countries of the Occident in world or even regional power. The sacrifices of war and her role as a bastion of the West in peace have entitled her to substantial postwar aid from the United States and Canada. But with her socialized economy such assistance has, to the broad mass of her people, been less of an animating goad than a cushion to lull the brooding sense of the precarious—that awareness not only of the kind of crisis world in which they live but of their own altered situation within it.

The birth of the League of Nations raised hope among men, and its rebirth through the United Nations has renewed that hope. But the most enduring major accomplishment of modern diplomacy was the prior establishment during the past half century of Anglo-American friendship. For if that had not been attained, there might never have been the wartime victories of which the peactime trophies have been these two world institutions. Yet Anglo-American understanding has come from facing the acerbities of a high-spirited family relationship rather than from evading them. No prim, disembodied, passionless ghost, it is, despite postprandial goodwill rhetoricians, a creature of flesh and blood to be tamed afresh in every epoch. Sir Stafford Cripps may have clashed with the American governors of the Economic Cooperation Administration, but neither did John Hay and Joseph Chamberlain, Sir Wilfrid Laurier, Lord Lansdowne and Theodore Roosevelt, Woodrow Wilson and David Lloyd George, Arthur Balfour and Charles Evans Hughes, Henry Stimson and Sir John Simon always pull their punches. For the more the English-speaking peoples must stick together, the more they may disagree, except in final emergencies, over how it should be done. What in final emergencies they do do together is what counts.

The likelihood of such an emergency arising between East and West has, for the moment, been abated by the West's own preponderant unity. But with the ebbing prospect of an early climax in that perpetual crisis, and with any economic recession at home, the American people may weary of their Sisyphean expenditures in Britain and western Europe. Yet if Britain had to fend economically all for herself or, as a closed economy, had of necessity to deal as such more and more closely with Soviet closed economies, her current bickerings with the United States could take a serious turn. So long as she is a counterpoise, His Majesty's loyal opposition, within the West itself, to the will of the United States, we can have an inner distribution of power which is a healthy one. Economically, too, East-West trade could normalize the commerce of Europe—and Asia—if it does not cause any of us to lower our guard politically or to forget that Soviet methods, but not Soviet objectives, vary. For Russia, ascertaining that head-on frontal pressure serves but to weld the Atlantic Alliance together, might seek to relax it by an oblique approach—by curtailing short-range crises so as ultimately to prevail in the long-range one.

The British people, on the other hand, do not want to be in the position of a bankrupt whom creditors keep in business lest a crash bring ruin to all. Overseas assistance has been warranted by their past contributions to the defense of civilized society. And though they can never repay in dollars, there is the undevaluated coin of statesmanship in which such debts may always be discharged.

When Franklin Roosevelt and Winston Churchill reaffirmed Anglo-American unison, they put it back on a plane from which they could command together the hearts and minds of free men everywhere. From that peak of common endeavor it was bound to descend. Yet it must function on high ground or not function at all. On lesser issues the United States and Britain may differ; the unity for which they must strive is a unity of principle. Nor can their unity exist for its own sake. The tradition of freedom which they share has a double utility. Employed domestically as a magnet to draw others to them, it may strengthen thereby their power for freedom, the freedom of humanity; but manifested also in concerted action, their heritage of liberty is the prerequisite of any deeper alliance which must vivify their less abstract political bond. At the inception of Anglo-American friendship more than five decades ago, its founders perceived that to stand together their peoples would have to stand side by side in support of great causes. Twice in war, belatedly yet magnificently, they were to do this; had they done it during the last peace there would not have been another such war. Fortified in the main through the joint power of the English-speaking peoples, the preponderance of the West should be to all who cherish liberty a practical means to a moral end. But statesmanship is the art of turning precept into performance, and without statesmanship we are doomed.

6

POWER OR SUBMISSION

The Problem of Government

As the alternative to submission, peace by power remains a cosmic safeguard. What it gives is a reprieve from war; tyranny deferred; a breathing space in which the West may organize itself if it can; a respite in which to work out institutions whose purposes are a better, freer, more abundant life for larger numbers everywhere. Yet proponents of federal world government are almost as dissatisfied with the consolidating strength of the West as the power politicians of the Kremlin whose expanding power in Europe it has arrested. Not that they are kindred spirits. The realists of Moscow, who regard themselves as idealists, and our own utopians, who fancy themselves to be realists, happen to pass each other on the same road as they proceed in opposite directions. For the contest of power is not extinguished by the preponderance of the West; the perpetual crisis of our time is merely alleviated, ringed around, and kept by it within bounds. When the West, drowning out the double talk of ideological warfare, speaks to Russia in the language of power, the idiom is her own; understanding it, she can adjust her policies accordingly. But since the East-West schism thus persists, so does the fundamental insecurity of a split world in the air-atomic age.

Can this be more fully dispelled? Various expedients have been suggested—world federal government, federal unions of the Atlantic basin or the European continent, amendments to the Charter of the

United Nations, or further agreements between some of its signatories. But would any of these, where and if practicable, bridge
the gulf between East and West? Or would they serve, instead, to
tighten the West's own political unity? To attain peace without
liberty, no effort is required. That we can ever get peace with
liberty but without preponderant power has yet to be demonstrated.

Abandon national sovereignties, it is nevertheless argued, and
you abolish major wars. The most elaborate of the solutions envisaged is to federate national units in one overriding world sovereignty. And this close-knit union, unlike the League of Nations
or the United Nations, would not be a league of states—though
national states will still possess local and domestic jurisdiction—but
a government to which each world citizen owes individual allegiance and on whom it can exercise direct authority. Sometimes it is
contended that member nations might only have to surrender limited powers to the wider union. To do the most important of tasks,
however, no line can be drawn which does not shift from the nation
to the federation the main powers of government. Constitutional
problems may or may not be a stumbling block. A basic question of
politics must be answered before they are even tackled. Many are
the sources of the world's malaise, but it is only East-West tension
which might be inflamed and which might exacerbate other ailments
to a fatal degree. Yet what is a remedy worth if, like this one, it cannot be administered or, if half applied, should prove worse than the
disease? For if Great Powers such as Russia and the United States,
while entering a world government, retained key portions of their
national sovereignty, the federal union would be one in name only;
in enforcing world law upon either of them, it would unloose upon
us all the very cataclysm it is designed to avert. When weapons
were so much less devastating, the American Federal Union was for
similar reasons rent by an irrepressible conflict. During the second
half of the twentieth century, and in even a cause as noble, could
all mankind afford another Civil War? The fact is that none of the
major states will cede vital rights and Russia—with whose muzzled

populace we cannot get into touch to discuss these notions—least of any.

The contest of power, since there can be no true world federation to absorb it, thus continues. The central malady of our time is the East-West crisis; world government, with Russia refusing to take the cure, cannot heal it. Theoretically, of course, a supranational government could still be set up from which only Russia and her satellite countries abstain. And if this were feasible on other grounds, it might further reinsure the preponderance of the West. But even so, even if one could be established, that would signify a constitutional reinforcement of sectional power rather than a total pooling of universal power. World tranquillization through world government must still be far to seek. As a Wellsian improvement of the public order, there is no doubt everything to be said for it. As an all-inclusive solution of the East-West schism, it is a benign yet irrelevant hoax.

For the Soviet Union, while a paladin of revolutionary internationalism against the national interests of others, is in itself, and without more than superficial incongruity, ultranationalistic and counterrevolutionary. To be anything else, to allow its internationalist ideology to serve any but a national and imperial Russian objective, would be to undermine its own *status quo*, its own totalitarian structure—its dictatorship of class, party, group, committee, or person. Yet no federal system—world, Atlantic, or European—can be conceived by us which is not founded on representative (congressional or parliamentary) democracy. The request which the movement for world government has to make of the Politburo is then majestic in its simplicity: all it asks is that at our bidding they overhaul Soviet politics and Russian society; that the Communist élite help us stop the world power contest by voluntarily relinquishing its own domestic power. The Russia of czars and commissars has, however, never been the self-abnegating Russia of Tolstoy. Ultimately change may have to come there, as before, through revolution; a spontaneous renunciation to meet the urgencies of the hour in world affairs is an idle dream. Yet without one,

without the demise of single-party rule, without human rights and
political freedom, in Russia as elsewhere, we can have no democratic world federation based on the civic responsibility of each
individual within it. Not that Russia is the sole obstacle to such a
union. But to the peoples of Western democracies the defects and
dangers of national sovereignty are not a closed book; they can
decide for themselves whether they want it cut down and to what
extent. Yet even if we did away with all of ours, even if our world
were reduced to but two monster sovereignties, Leviathans of the
East and West, we should still need to stay on top lest liberty go
under, still require that the preponderance of the free underpin any
union of the free.

To Communist belief that wars come from the clash of monopoly capitalism, to the plain man's revulsion against international
cartels which put profits before country, the new federalists would
probably retort that national sovereignty is the tool which these
and other sinister forces—of racial myth and fascist doctrine, of
greed and power—manipulate. It must in their view always be absolute by nature and can therefore neither be controlled nor cur-
tailed; to achieve a permanent peace we shall have to rid ourselves
of national sovereignty outright. *Écrasez l'infâme!* Yet they have
never proposed machinery which other than on paper could carry
out the mission contemplated. Most of Central and eastern Europe,
quite apart from German and Russian despotism, has no tradition
of representative democracy, and neither have the majority of Latin
Americans. What, too, about the backward peoples of Asia and
Africa, even those who have won their national liberty—by what
method, before they have learned how to conduct in freedom their
own affairs of state, are they suddenly to adapt themselves to any
genuinely representative world system? What, furthermore, would
be the destiny of the West if representation by population made the
East dominant in a world parliament; what would be the fate of
the Occident if within it, through strength of numbers rather than
effective power, the Orient held sway? So as to equalize power
with numbers, so as to counteract any uniform counting of heads,

the dubious mechanism of weighted voting by nations or regions has been suggested. But would that not infringe upon the strict federalist principle of direct, unmediated representation of the individual?

Details such as these are not minor ones. Any larger federation must differ from a league of states as a patchwork quilt differs from a seamless web. It cannot cooperate, aloofly or intimately, with a cluster of sovereignties; all of their economies it must fuse integrally together as one. Neofederalist blueprints may attempt to mark off security from the rest of public affairs, to separate in legislation and administration the local, the national, and the world-wide. Divisions of that sort would be unreal in theory and untenable in practice. Between the internal and the external, between domestic and foreign policy, watertight compartments are no longer possible. And if a world federal scheme broke down under the dead-weight of an overcentralized bureaucracy or perished from "the curse of bigness," civilization itself might suffer.

Even a federation of the Atlantic democracies, while less grandiose in concept than one of the entire world or one of the entire non-Soviet world, might collapse from elephantiasis in politics. Yet credit should go to its advocates because they at least realize that the spirit which unifies federal unions within some nations is absent between most of them. For the peoples of the world cannot have a common world sovereignty until they have a common world aim— an aim not of peace in the abstract but of a world order in which the chief nations concur. The vision of world government is one of peace by consent; unavowed yet implicit in other schemes of a wider federal union is the reality of peace by power. An Atlantic federation might divert the contest of power from the perpendicular rivalries of some member states to more horizontal pressures and counterpressures in the social and economic spheres; but it would mitigate any inner struggle between selected sovereignties of the West only to fortify over against the East its own balance of power. Through disunion, the Atlantic peoples twice permitted war to be thrust upon us; through their more formal unity at last, through the Atlantic Alliance, the hazards of its recurrence are this time being less slothfully repulsed. But there might also be too organic a link, a connection which stifles where looser ties of mutual aid and concerted strategies can more effectually bind.

Federal unions such as the American, the Swiss, the Canadian, the Australian, were formed by states which shared not only a common moral purpose but a common technique of government. And while the sentiment of nationality suffuses each with a sense of fellowship—one that is lacking in broader schemes—each of these merged sovereignties has had an immediate utility. For they are instruments of direct rule and administration; as such they are neither inoperable politically by the free peoples which established them, nor geographically unmanageable within any territorial area to which they could stretch. Air communication may telescope some kinds of continental and intracontinental traffic; the shattering of immemorial barriers of space and time has, in our age of atomic-hydrogen bombs, guided missiles, and biological warfare, frightened us all. Yet a world society whose channels of business—railways, highways, ships at sea—still run so predominantly on the earth's surface, is also one for whom independent sovereignties are still the normal, regulatory mainstays of the life of man. Through history and migration, culture and interest, an oceanic expanse such as the North Atlantic unites those who dwell on both of its shores. Through too intimate a union—with its differing nationalities rubbing each other, in the daily affairs of a close-knit community, the wrong way—even it could as chaotically divide.

A conflict of powers between the center and the separate states is, as the scope of domestic government increases, a feature of modern federations. And of necessity the drift in them is toward the center. That conflict occurs, however, within relatively homogeneous nations or within regions which may be as unified politically on land as they would be riven demographically, economically, administratively by sea; where the forfeiture of powers can be an extension of government and not its impairment. For across oceans, between distant continents, and among heterogeneous if like-minded peoples, a federal relationship would tend not only toward less rather than more efficiency but toward an ill will which must vitiate the union itself. By overdoing the unity of the West we can thus undo its preponderance. In the long future, the nature, the inventions, and the governance of men may one day be less out of joint with each other. Meanwhile, the constitutional limitations which American sovereignty has imposed on the Atlantic Alliance reveal how far we are from converting it into a full-blown federation. The panaceas of tomorrow are no therapy for the fevers of today. But as our patient's strength is now built up, he should with our assistance be able to hold his own.

Yet even within an area as geographically coherent as non-Soviet Europe, national sovereignty must, like Charles II of England, take an unconscionable time a-dying. That you can have a common citizenship without a common language, Switzerland, Canada, and South Africa have shown; but in Europe as a whole there are economic and political barriers to be surmounted which earlier, simpler, or younger federations did not face. The Council of Europe, with its ministerial executive committee and its public advisory consultative assembly, can do things in unison which would signify a regional abatement of sovereignty. Federal in cooperative purposes it may tend to be; in composition, its constituency being one of governments and parliaments rather than of individual Europeans, it is still national. Yet within its more restricted and less unwieldy sphere, so advanced a league of states may be able to carry its pragmatic internationalism further than the United Nations itself. Time will tell.

Perhaps the unity of Europe can, like an appetite, grow as it is fed. Psychologically, the Atlantic Pact as a measure of security, by giving Europe more freedom from fear or less fear for its freedom, is a spur to confidence, a stimulus thereby to recovery. As the Council of Europe spreads its wings, the Organization for European Economic Cooperation, which represents the beneficiaries of American aid, should come under them. Economically, the Council of Europe will never acquire the attributes of a federation until it switches from currency controls to a single currency, from tariffs, quotas, and passports to freedom of trade and travel. But whether a customs union would be a forerunner of political union or a sequel to it, a lot may be accomplished through specific rather than general agreements to improve functionally a situation which each government alone cannot improve. For tariffs are not so much an obstacle to union as other differences—in social welfare legislation, in fixed wages, and in supported price structures—which exist between various controlled economies.

The concept of a United States of Europe is a formula for success which fascinates public men born and bred in the United States of America. But it would be self-defeating if, as a condition for the continuance of economic aid to friends and allies, they were to insist that the Council of Europe recast itself into a federal union like their own. There is no doubt that unless European countries act together, they will become accustomed to living indefinitely on an American dole. Incentives to self-help are needed. But the objectives of the European Recovery Program were neither wholly altruistic nor, even where self-interested, confined to the long-run stake of the American economy in the prosperity of others. It was launched during the East-West crisis, when the national strength or social fabric of countries racked by war and aligned with us had to be preserved. The world balance would have shifted adversely if all Europe, with or without Britain, had fallen into the Soviet orbit; the odds against war itself might have decreased as a more flimsy equalization of power between East and West served to replace the preponderance of the West. And if the Atlantic Alliance is strategic reinsurance against so dire a contingency, the European Recovery Program complements it in other essential spheres.

Tact for circumstance, the quality in leadership of knowing when to sit back no less than when to drive ahead, is one that the United States must learn through trial and error. The occasions are many when candor from Washington is the hope of the free world; but the United States, to sustain the moral authority on which her political and economic authority must rest, will have to seek among her Allies and associates not so much a minimum of accord as a maximum of assent. If none of them—neither she nor the others— can enter a global or Atlantic federation, it may also be unfeasible for some of them to join a European federal union. On that issue American and French public men seem to be nearest in their views; a United States of Europe might, they feel, have precluded Europe's recurrent wars, or prevent a civil war of its own. Yet no European federation was needed to save the last peace. It could have been done through existing agencies; until too late men lacked the will, not the means. For the fragmentation was not one of a continent but of Western society, and less one of Western society than of its ethos. The disunity of Europe, lamentable though it be, proved to be no more at fault than the working estrangement of Britain and the United States from each other and of the English-speaking peoples from France. Vivid to some of us at the time, the lesson of those years is diplomatic and strategic rather than constitutional—one not of powers but of power. And it is a lesson we will again ignore at our peril.

Meanwhile, even economically the Council of Europe cannot provide continental or semicontinental answers to questions that are world-wide in scale and character. Better than a policy of beggar-my-neighbor is one of taking in each other's washing—or of trying to do more of everybody's together. Smaller combinations such as Benelux, Italy and France, an Anglo-Scandinavian grouping, may yet be nuclei for experiments that raze national economic boundaries, that foster interchange of goods and mass production. But not since it became a trader and manufacturer has Europe been self-sufficient or self-supporting. Dollar scarcity for the purchase of raw materials, the loss of markets for what these produce, comes, moreover, at a moment when foreign investments have gone down and there is the pressure of an increased population at home against the means of subsistence. Europe's economic decline, the rise of industrial competition overseas, which had been under way since the end of the nineteenth century, two world wars accelerated. Aid from the New World may have eased the postwar shock; belts which have been drawn cruelly tight for most might have to be drawn tight for all; more common action is necessary under any circumstances. But the European Recovery Program itself and President Truman's subsequent proposal for the capital and technological development of undeveloped lands illustrate that Europe's own economic unity will, for a number of years, have to be supplemented by other far-reaching endeavors. And even ventures as important as these must be coordinated with the demands upon human and material resources of postwar rearmament. For in Europe, as in world affairs as a whole, the East-West contest, which renders common economic efforts more urgent, impedes at the same time their complete and early fulfillment.

But Europe is not only beset by that intermingling of power politics and power economics which is the hallmark of our epoch. Some of the specific difficulties which block the path of any continental or quasi-continental federation are as serious as the general ones. How, for example, could the colonial possessions of its component states be fitted into a project which would have to be based on geographic proximity, on a common level of culture, and on the same aptitude for representative democracy; one which is to be not a league of national units but a federal union of free individuals? France might argue that on such grounds none may object to the inclusion of her North African territories; yet even about them others would not be sure. The fact is, of course, that no subordinate position will be accepted anywhere nowadays by overseas dependencies which can strike out for themselves. As for the rest, those which under modern conditions cannot go their own way, they would have to be transferred, in the event of a European union, from their present rulers to a joint federal suzerainty. For you cannot surrender national sovereignty at home and yet retain it, as the overlord of subject peoples, abroad. If former colonies became trusteeships of the United Nations, the federation of Europe could, under the Charter, be their administering authority. But they might cease, thereby, in any direct or immediate sense, to be overseas props of the domestic economic recovery of particular European countries.

And that is an aspect of the world crisis which no federal reallocation of colonies can neglect.

True of others, this is peculiarly so as it affects the power of Britain. Oceanic rather than insular, world-wide rather than continental, much of her strength is, nevertheless, not colonial in origin but emanates from voluntary ties with Commonwealth sovereignties overseas. Neither politically nor economically could their historic fellowship remain unaltered by the entry of Britain into a European federation, into the sort of close union which the self-governing Dominions of the old Empire were never able to forge between themselves. Preferential tariffs have contributed so considerably to the national economy of each Commonwealth country that they cannot be done away with unless broader commercial arrangements offer satisfactory equivalents. From Britain's own colonial possessions, moreover, sterling-area advantages in the purchase of raw materials and in the sale of manufactures might vanish, if they had to be shared not only with other colonial Powers which could reciprocate wholly or in part, but with every state of the European union. No federal scheme, at any rate, can be entertained which would not provide for the productivity of Britain's large populace—a nation whose costly experiments in social betterment coincide with her unprecedented financial impoverishment. Anything else must add to the burdens of a united Europe and not detract from them. In no other fashion can Britain pull her weight as an Atlantic Ally in the defense of the West.

A European union which saps the foundations of British power might wreck its own. In the Battle of the Pound, or in the quest for dollars, a chasm yawns between Britain's planned austerities, with the accent on more exports and fewer imports, and the goals of her less autarchic continental associates. Such, however, is the paradox of her relations with them that while one foot is, as always, out of Europe, the other foot has never been planted as firmly within it. The Council of Europe cannot, with Britain as a member, be integrated federally. Yet only by including her can it be sound economically and viable strategically.

Nor might Germans safely be dealt with in any federation of Europe—not, at any rate, unless the British also could take part. Time after time the majority French view of how to treat Germans has, at history's blood-stained bar, been vindicated. Constrained to acquiesce in an Anglo-American revival of western Germany, the French now feel that such an event may portend less risk if the new Teutonic state were admitted to a continental federation; if the molten lava of a sovereign Germanism were cooled and diluted by being poured into a common European mold. Yet as a self-infatuated racial entity the Germans might, when the chance beckoned, doff a federal mask, regroup with eastern and other Teutonic brethren, and become the national element within the federation which is numerically, industrially, and militarily supreme. And then, having been more fully rehabilitated by us, they may again join forces with Russia to dominate not Europe alone but mankind. The fruits of victory which we had wrested from Germany at the front door we should thus return to her at the back. The unity of Europe would be achieved, as it was almost achieved by arms twice before in this century—but not as a federal representative democracy nor as a bulwark of the West.

Meanwhile, regional or special pacts, European, Atlantic, inter-American, have been knitting together, within the ambit of the United Nations, key sectors of our society. A broader agreement of a similar character has been propounded as one that might more properly subserve the universal aims of the world organization. Long before the San Francisco Conference it had been observed that the directing concert of victor Great Powers must be to the United Nations as the spinal cord is to the human body. Between wars right without might had been impotent; peace by power meant that these henceforth should be as one. But would they? And what if Great Powers were at variance on the morrow as they had been on the eve of conflict? Then other groupings, truly regional or masquerading as such, must ensue until collective security can, under the United Nations, be more collective and less insecure.

In its peace-keeping and other tasks the Security Council has

been thwarted by the right of veto which the Charter accords to
its five permanent members. The abuse of the veto is, however, but
a phase of the deeper East-West contest—one which also involves
issues arising from the war and which, as such, were not supposed
to come before it. East-West rivalry underlay the necessity for
intervention by the Security Council in Iran and Greece, though
not in Kashmir. Yet the inadequacies of major Powers seated in the
Security Council cannot always be attributed to the veto or the
East-West contest. Neither factor entered into the Palestine situation; over Indonesia the Communist shadow loomed only in the
background. Nevertheless dissent over the pacific settlement of disputes; the impasse over the regulation of conventional armaments
and the establishment of international police forces; the rejection by
Russia of Assembly proposals for world control of atomic energy;
disingenuousness on both sides over the admission of new members;
wrangles over what is and what is not a procedural question—all these
are symptoms of a perpetual crisis which has more than the Council
Chamber in its grip. Sovereignty in most of those fields the governments of the West may now be disposed to ameliorate; Russia clings
to the veto, through which it is expressed, so as to have a counter-
weight against their predominance in numbers and strength. Nor is
Peking likely to differ from Moscow about this. But even if some
abatement is obtained, none of the permanent members will abandon
a sovereign right to protect itself against sanctions, to nullify coercive action which might bring Great Powers to blows, to ward off
under the Charter a world war in the name of the Charter.

A setting for the power struggle, the United Nations is itself
organized as a hierarchy of power. Yet the prerogatives within it
which Great Powers enjoy are but an index of the heavier burdens
they shoulder in war, the greater authority they must bear for the
maintenance of peace. Without them there would be no corrective
to sovereign rights voiced within the organization by minor states,
some of whom—protégés of both the East and the West—are not
qualified to belong and many of whom have little or no capacity to
contribute. It is, if any, the Middle Powers which could nourish a

grievance against an informal system of representation in the Security Council by geographical or political blocs. For doing much more than their lesser confrères, they possess no privileges over and beyond theirs—although under Article 23 of the Charter due regard was to be specially paid to such claims in the election to the Security Council of nonpermanent members. For here, as elsewhere, it is the task of the United Nations to correlate the sovereignty of the many with the power of the few and the power of the few with each other.

To the Soviet Union's network of regional pacts the West has been responding with a series of its own. Some non-Communist experts agree with Moscow that the Atlantic Alliance contravenes the Charter. The Supreme Court, said Mr. Dooley, follows the election returns and it is not astonishing when each country's interpretation of law is colored by exigencies of policy.

Can the veto be by-passed without by-passing, in the enforcement of peace, the Security Council as a whole? All members who wish the deadlocked machinery to be implemented and are willing to prepare in common against the threat or fact of aggression may, as the Charter specifies, band themselves together under the collective right of self-defense (Article 51; also Articles 52 to 54). If Great Powers within such a broad subsidiary grouping voluntarily circumscribe their own exercise of the veto, it might be of some value. But that grouping, too, would still be unable to subject to the paramount jurisdiction of the Security Council any serious problem which Russia desired, later or at once, to exclude; it could not break that world stalemate which the East-West contest has bred. Nor is it plausible to argue that, since the Soviet Union itself might adhere, Moscow cannot complain about a general pact designed to circumvent its own veto right. The European Recovery Program, which Russia opposed so strenuously, was likewise open to her and her satellites. Obviously, if the Soviet Union were disposed to sign a special protocol of that sort, it would not have been necessary to devise one in the first place. Yet her abstention might convert the entire United Nations into one vast anti-Soviet combine, a body which would be even less useful politically than it is now and strategically no more effectual.

For this might not only leave statecraft with fewer strings to its bow. The remaining ones would also be less taut. Of all the Powers of the West, the signatories of the Atlantic Alliance are those best suited to take the lead as a solid, coherent, regional group for collective self-defense under the Charter. No General Staff, inside or outside the United Nations, can plan with its opposite numbers to meet every strategic need. Specific contingencies call for specific preparations; only between those who carry a precise operational responsibility can, for reasons of secrecy and efficiency, participation be shared. To ensure the preponderance of the West, any who thus join together must rely on other like-minded nations to stand at their side or come to their support. But in that pact of mutual assistance which should be its core, the breadth of mutuality cannot outrun the faculty of assistance.

Diplomatically, also, the narrower defensive pact might be an instrumentality through which we may work without driving the Soviet Union back into complete isolation. For the Atlantic Powers are merely doing within their own sphere what Russia has already done in hers; between them lies the larger proportion of the United Nations membership committed and encumbered neither more nor less than before. And as long as the Soviet Union takes part with its Eastern bloc in that organization's main proceedings, the United Nations may somehow persevere in the province of mediation and conciliation—especially if other issues should supervene on which the East-West contest does not wholly impinge. The United Nations functions, above all, as a bridge, barricaded though it be at one end, across which East-West traffic still trickles; a span over which communications may yet increase if, through counter-pressure from the West, the world struggle relaxes. Does Russia stay within the organization so as to sabotage its labors? Even if that were the case, we should welcome her departure only if the residuum were thus rendered more competent to enforce its own will. But in her absence the East-West contest would continue elsewhere as before. And

this being so, there must still be resort to those exterior power expedients—the Brussels Treaty, the North Atlantic Pact—which the
Russian challenge has evoked.

Within the confines of world rivalry the United Nations is, besides, a point of origin for international welfare politics as expressed
through the General Assembly, the Trusteeship Council, and the
Economic and Social Council. Through its specialized agencies, and
despite their virtual boycott by the Soviet Union, it is a clearing
house for constructive nonpolitical undertakings. The Declaration
of Human Rights and the Genocide Convention restate civilized
ideals; as such they are touchstones by which members of the United
Nations should abide. But welfare politics cannot determine basic
issues through which they themselves are shaped; what they might do
is revise and ameliorate an order of peace which power factors direct
and sustain. As the power struggle is moderated, the United Nations
may yet steer between two absolutes, between that Scylla of the
past which is absolute national sovereignty and that Charybdis of
the future which is absolute world sovereignty, to an empirical internationalism of relative sovereignty. Differences in economic systems
are, moreover, another rock on which it could founder. And it is
as the highest common denominator between systems and sovereignties alike that the United Nations has its work cut out for it.

A mechanism whose chief propulsion must be supplied by member
governments, its defects are our own. Proposals to focus more power
within it or within an entirely federalized organization have been
assessed in these pages on grounds of their practicability or imprac-
ticability. Yet an observation of trends within the appropriate organ
of the United Nations itself might raise doubts not only of their
feasibility but of their wisdom. For the peace which preserves freedom can also stifle it. In the affirmation of liberty resides the justifi-
cation of power. But even when it could, even in instances when
it was not hobbled by its own rules or the East-West feud, the
Security Council has not borne witness to that central truth. We
must beware lest as an antidote to dynamic national dictatorships it
itself becomes a sluggish international one. A strait-jacket for those

who live by force, a more concentrated world authority would first also have to be a safety valve for living forces. The goads of crisis may alert the major chancelleries of the West to the moral as well as the material requisites of leadership. But would they again grow slack if the contest of power slowed down or hung fire?

Within the United Nations itself, as is exemplified by the contrast between the General Assembly, which cannot act, and the Security Council, which should, the veto is not the whole story. As counterirritants, if not as institutional checks and balances, we must look to the more enlightened among small and Middle Powers when the responsibility which Great Powers possess is muddled by ignorance, collusion, or arbitrary caprice. In any inner contest of power it is therefore the national sovereignty which they retain that enables them to be mouthpieces of liberty, repositories of a statesmanship which might not otherwise come independently to the fore —one that is as good as that of more populous nations, or better. For if a collectivity of power is needed to protect freedom, liberty may also repose in its diffusion. Just as the preponderance of the West is a world counterpoise to monopoly by the East, so within any international organization redress against a monopoly of power must be assured. Only between the systole of power and the diastole of liberty will the heart of the United Nations beat as it ought.

The machinery of the United Nations, like that of the League of Nations before it, has never had a fair chance to show what it can do. Expected to start with a clean slate, it was designed not to settle the war but to preserve the peace. In an imperfect world, however, the best laid schemes of mice and men often go amiss; the uninterrupted struggle for power, subdued through bloodshed between one set of contestants, exacerbated through diplomacy between another, cuts across so neat a parceling out of duties, so well defined a division of the indivisible. An offshoot of the struggle, the United Nations emerged in an hour of equilibrium, at a transient moment in the heat of common victory, when East-West relations were still malleable, before the new postwar configurations had congealed. The row it has to hoe is a harder one than was anticipated; in their season the seeds planted will ripen and bloom. But the United Nations cannot, through its own decrees, terminate the contest of power. The contest of power will instead make or mar the United Nations.

In other words the more the West stands firm, the better the opportunity for a world order in which a more genuinely collective responsibility may prevail. Such also, perhaps, is the angle from which may be surveyed the East-West failure to agree upon the international control of atomic energy or to regulate conventional armaments. Since the proposals of the United Nations Atomic Energy Commission, which the General Assembly accepted by an overwhelming majority, provided for enforcement without veto, they were unacceptable to Russia. But the quarrel is, at bottom, not only over sovereignty, ownership, or timing: how violations are to be punished or how the two sides are to synchronize at each stage their respective contributions to the plan. Inspection and administration to be effective must elicit from the Soviet Union, as from all participants, a telling disclosure of its industrial, technological, and therefore military resources. And as its totalitarian structure is unveiled, it would of necessity be riveting itself cooperatively, interchangeably, and irrevocably to the more liberal economies of the West. Less and less could the regime thus fall back on secrecy as a strategy of the nation's power or its own; more than an abatement of sovereignty, Russian concurrence might herald a voluntary and involuntary modification of the Soviet system itself. Between the knout at home and the *niet* abroad, the nexus has been plain.

After 1919, the same generation which thought war could be outlawed by solemn interdict also believed that in paper agreements of arms limitation there was some magic efficacy. Nor was it jolted from its dogmatic slumbers when nations arose which scorned peace by pact—which derided the sanctity of treaties and scoffed at the validity of pacifism. For war would come, the West now muttered in the wishful innocence of its sleep, not from what these may say or do but from any competition which we ourselves might offer them. The martial and political supremacy we had purchased so dearly between 1914–1918 we therefore let crumble. We refused to identify evil as such, or, if we did, we fancied that to turn our backs was to banish it. Counters we held in the game of world politics we even helped some to redirect against ourselves.

Yet since between two sides there can, in the seesaw of power, be no equipoise that is lasting or exact, power which might erupt may only be stabilized when more power is amassed against it. Never again should we lose from sight the brute fact that a treaty of arms regulation or limitation reflects and registers but does not blot out the dynamics of power; that among friends, when fundamentals in policy converge rather than collide, accumulations of arms either subside or should be concerted against an opposing camp. The way to stop an arms race is not to treat allies and antagonists alike, not for some to abstain or for each to run in it by himself, but to combine with others who share a common goal. For the greater the power of the West, the less the likelihood that in any final or cataclysmic sense it will ever have to be used.

One thing which distinguishes the East-West schism from the preceding world rivalry should also be noted. Nazism may have constituted an atavistic renunciation by the German people of the civilized West; Communism has become a world-wide Russian conspiracy to control it. Between the two threats to the freedom of others there can be little to choose. But for all her chauvinism Russia is not incited by an ideology of race, a *mystique* of tribal self-idolatry, a thunderous Wagnerian lunacy in which the twilight of the gods is the destructive prologue to a barbaric phantasmagoria of eternal night. Coolly and with detachment, if the Kremlin perceives that further competitive effort will not pay, some *modus vivendi* with it may be feasible.

More than that is unlikely. Any comprehensive, all-round settlement is bound to be remote when the abstract and the concrete are so politically mixed up. What might be tried are provisional accommodations over specific points of detail. Nor would the case for such an eventual approach require endorsement through ominous analogies out of a distant past; from the manner in which

Christians and Moslems, Protestants and Catholics had to spill each other's blood before they delimited their conflicts of doctrine by each recognizing the limits of their power. Negatively, at any rate, we need not go beyond the coming of the war of 1939 to illustrate the crucial role in peace-keeping of the particular rather than the general. For when some among us assisted or permitted Germans to violate the Treaty of Versailles, we ourselves did more to ruin the last peace settlement than any remissness elsewhere in enforcing or in reinforcing the Covenant of the League of Nations. The loudest in pointing to the infirmities of the general peace machinery were thus often those who simultaneously did most to undermine the very order of power on which it rested.

Yet if that lesson has been learned, and if intracontinental war is thereby averted, the common danger might bring about a working agreement to differ. Guarantees, however, for a *modus vivendi* between East and West must themselves still be furnished by factors of mutually counteracting power—on the sanction of force which each side marshals behind it and on the extent to which its vexed and uneasy maintenance will further correspond to their evident national interests.

If the means are precarious, the ends are complex. For it is not enough to lift the curse of war; what we want is not peace alone but peace with freedom. The reconciliation of liberty with security may be the inmost quest of modern democracies. When translated into the domain of world affairs, it is one which by itself would suffice to prolong uncertainty and postpone the establishment of any more foolproof system of peace. You may win or lose in the contest of power; to it there is, alas, no effortless alternative, from it no painless self-exemption; as it proceeds without surcease, few countries in the West can be so aloof as to remain unaffected by it. Yet would-be architects of a nobler edifice for humanity are apt to forget that blueprints are futile when you have been robbed of your title deeds or when trespassers have seized your land. Nor do they recall that unless the power of an idea is harnessed to the idea of power, the best may well become the enemy of the good.

Peace by power is, in an age of tension, no recipe for peace of mind. But from other elements in its calculus of strength should not be omitted that stoic power of endurance and self-renewal, that mingled resiliency and abiding faith, which is nothing less than the will to live and which, when given a chance, free men and free societies display invincibly. A gift above price, this is the moral quality which enables them to master crisis as they are inured to it—and one which must embolden them in time, if their limbs are strong, their hearts stout, their vision clear, to resume, harassed, perplexed, yet undaunted, their long-retarded onward march.

INDEX